Better Homes and Gardens®

Perennials

You Can Grow

© 1978 by Meredith Corporation, Des Moines, Iowa. All Rights Reserved.
Printed in the United States of America. First Edition. First Printing.
Library of Congress Catalog Card Number: 77-085884
ISBN: 0-696-00280-9

**BETTER HOMES AND
GARDENS BOOKS**

Editor: Gerald Knox
Art Director:
  Ernest Shelton
Associate Art Director:
  Randall Yontz
Production and
Copy Editors:
  David Kirchner
  Paul S. Kitzke
Garden and Outdoor
Living Editor:
  Beverly Garrett
Garden Book Editor:
  Steven Coulter
Associate Garden Editor:
  Douglas Jimerson
Perennials You Can Grow
Editor: Kay Stroud
Senior Graphic Designer:
  Harijs Priekulis
Graphic Designers:
  Faith Berven
  Sheryl Veenschoten
  Richard Lewis
  Neoma Alt West

CONTENTS

Perennials and Biennials

No one knows quite how long ago the love for gardening was first felt by human beings; but we do know that in America, the early settlers from England brought with them seeds and roots of well-loved plants to grow in colonial gardens.

In the years since, gardens have never ceased to fascinate Americans as the frontier pushed ever westward, at last to the Pacific Ocean and a climate far different from that of New England, where frigid winters were a real threat.

In a country as vast as ours, what may be a perennial plant in one area may not be so in another. But nowhere in America is there a lack of perennial plants that can serve as the backbone of a flower border. In zones 9 and 10, these may well differ widely from the hardy perennials counted upon to appear year after year in Northern zones.

The first thing a beginning gardener should do is to study a zonal map (see pages 92 and 93) then look for plants suited to his climate. Or, if you're an experienced gardener confronted by a need to move— something that often

happens in this ever-mobile world in which we live— it's time to seek new plants that will take the place of older friends and rediscover the fun and excitement of learning to garden well under a new group of climatic conditions, seasons for planting and bloom, different types of soil, and annual expected amount of rainfall. These are just a few of the factors you should take into account as you do perennial planting plans. Wherever you live, it pays to understand your climate.

Biennials are usually described as plants that bloom the year following their sowing, then die. But as you will learn on the pages to follow, many of the biennials often

self-sow so cheerfully that they behave like perennials in many climates. Several of them—foxglove, hollyhocks, Canterbury bells—are graceful verticals whose height can lend distinction to the back-of-the-border area in your garden.

Taken together, the plant group we know as perennials and biennials can give you great joy with little work and combine beautifully with annuals—amiable plants also deserving of your admiration.

Thus far, the main role of perennials here discussed has been as valuable members of flowering borders. But there are many plants within the group that play other roles as well —ground covers in sun or shade; color in rock gardens; bouquets to take into the house; heralds of spring from hardy bulbs and native wildflowers; and exotic tufts produced by ornamental grasses. Each of these uses of perennials will be discussed in later sections of this book.

One of the major factors determining success or failure with perennials—other than zonal hardiness which has already been discussed —is quality of soil and advance preparation of a bed. Have a soil test made before you begin setting out plants. Usually your state's agricultural college or its extension services will do this for you. Only then can you learn the pH factor of the soil and if it is necessary to sweeten a too-acid soil or add acid to an overly alkaline soil.

Preparation in advance of planting can't be over-rated. For small areas this can be done with a spade by digging down 12 to 24 inches, thoroughly cultivating soil as you go, then adding whatever's necessary: coarse sand and small gravel, peat moss, well-rotted manure, bone

meal, and balanced fertilizer are possibilities. Someone has said: "Always dig a $5 hole for a $1 plant." The basic meaning is clear: the better your preparation of a bed for a plant, the greater will be your rewards in its health, longevity, and productivity.

Plan to keep a garden diary, noting when and where you set out plants and recording dates of bloom over a number of seasons. And make a genuine effort to learn the botanical —as well as the common—names of your plants. So many plants of a variety of species are called by the same common name in various parts of the country that the only real way to know for certain what's growing in your garden is to learn its botanical name.

Finally, remember the old adage concerning perennials: the first year it sleeps; the second year it creeps; the third year it leaps. With this trite but true saying in mind, you'll find it easier to be patient with a perennial plant that takes off a bit slowly at first.

Using Perennials

Versatility is one of the qualities of hardy perennials that makes them so highly valued by flower gardeners everywhere. If you want bloom from earliest spring right up to killing frost, there are plants in the perennial family to do the job.

The photographs on these pages suggest some of the many ways in which perennials may be put to work: as edgings along garden paths; in mixed borders, perhaps combined in pleasing ways with annuals; in shady spots where you'd still like color; and in rock gardens as handsome partners to blooming shrubs and low-growing evergreens. Or, for a fragrant garden, look to perennials—some of them herbs—to perfume the air around you from narcissus-time until frost.

Massed plantings of sweet williams, calendulas, pinks, yellow and white violas, and azaleas form brilliant strips at either side of a garden path.

Rose-pink hardy phlox B. Symons-Jeune is in view at lower right foreground, along with baby's breath Bristol Fairy. Next to phlox is Cambridge Scarlet bee-balm with achillea Coronation Gold and gloriosa daisy. Back of these are semi-double Heliopsis scabra. To their left is lythrum Morden's Pink.

Mixing annuals and perennials lends an old-fashioned air to this border. Grouped are calendulas, sweet williams, pink Iceland poppies, and pansies.

Yellow-edged, large-leaf Siebold hosta (above) finds flattering companions in rudbeckia Goldstrum, white phlox, all in a shady spot between shrub plantings.

Looking as if Nature were the artist, this interesting rock garden is the result of careful design that turned a troublesome slope into a lovely sight. Pink mounds in foreground are creeping phlox. Rock cress bears the tiny white bloom (lower left). To its left is Hino-Crimson azalea, Miriam azalea (pink), and Delaware Valley White azalea. Tulips and daffodils outline the upper ledge. Primroses and Basket-of-Gold alyssum are the other colorful perennials that are in such pleasant contrast with the cool gray of stone and the green of several low-growing evergreens nearby.

For a drift of cool white bloom in June, choose cerastium, also called snow-in-summer. It's a spreader, so cut back each year to desired size. Plant in sun—it's drought tolerant. Zone 2.

Iris

The irresistible iris is undisputed queen of many perennial borders from spring on into early summer. The beginner is apt to think only of the tall bearded varieties such as Red Storm, shown above. But there are a large group of others in the tribe: early blooming dwarfs; Siberians; and spuria, which blooms after the bearded iris have closed for the season. Also late to bloom are Japanese iris with their unbelievably huge and upturned faces that measure up to 10 inches in diameter.

Plant spuria iris—this one's Dawn Candle—in rich, moist soil in full sun.

Japanese iris Driven Snow (white), Good Omen (purple), Stippled Ripples (variegated).

1 Clumps of bearded iris need to be dug up, divided, and replanted about every 3 years. Use a sharp knife to separate the rhizomes, and make sure each division has a strong section of roots.

2 After separating, clean, and trim off decayed or corky ends of rhizomes. Check for borers; cut them out. Trim the foliage to a fan shape.

3 Be sure to prepare the soil well before planting new divisions. Spade in plant food and compost. Place rhizome on a ridge of soil.

PERENNIAL FAVORITES
Peonies

Think peony, if you want a plant that's generous in rewarding you for minimal care. Once they're established for a year or two, you can count on armloads of bloom in spring. Fertilize after blooming.

Tree peonies like Kagura Jishi, shown above, don't die back each fall as do herbaceous types. The trees bloom earlier, also.

June Brilliant (herbaceous) truly glows.

Mercy, also herbaceous, is a single type.

1 While undisturbed peonies will often bloom faithfully for a century, it's good garden practice to lift and divide herbaceous peonies about once every 10 years. And this task can be done only in the fall.

First, dig a shallow trench just outside the edge of the clump. When plant is completely encircled, pry under root mass with a spade, as you lift from the top, using stems as a "handle" to pull with.

Use a hose to wash away all soil so you can see clearly where "eyes" are located on roots. This helps you to decide on how many sturdy divisions you should make. Making too many means a longer wait for bloom.

2 Use a sturdy, well-sharpened knife to make the divisions. No division should have fewer than 3 eyes; divisions having from 5 to 8 eyes are better, since newly set-out plants can be expected to perform well the following spring. It takes at least two years for 3-eye divisions to bloom significantly.

This is a fact worth remembering when buying new peony plants from a nurseryman. The difference in prices usually reflects the number of eyes your plant will have. Newer introductions will also cost more than the older favorites. Pick both early and late bloomers for a longer period of peony color in the spring.

3 To plant a new division, begin by digging a deep hole (2 feet) in a sunny location and replacing subsoil with fresh topsoil, unless subsoil in your area is exceptionally rich. To encourage sturdy growth, add humus and bone meal to soil you replace in hole. Do **not** use peat moss or cow manure, however.

Set divisions 3 feet apart. Be sure that eyes are 1 to 2 inches below soil surface—no more, no less. Measure to be sure. Spread roots over firm mound formed at bottom of hole. Fill with more topsoil and water in well. Fertilize after each season's bloom. In cold climate areas, mulch with 2 to 4 inches of straw or leaves.

PERENNIAL FAVORITES

Daylilies

The Greeks had a word for this summer star: Hemerocallis, meaning "beautiful for a day," and that describes well the plant's bloom schedule. Each stem will have from 5 to 10 buds; as one fades, another soon opens.

Modern hybridizers have developed varieties which bloom early, mid-season, and late— allowing you flowers from May on into the month of September.

Colors range from yellow through peach, orange, pink, mauve, and red. The delicate melon-color Ruth Lehman (36 in.), above, belongs to the mid-season bloom group.

There are numerous tall varieties—28 to 36 inches—that make perfect back-of-border plants. Others bloom at heights as low as 15 inches—suitable for mid- and front-of-border spots.

Showy trio: Shooting Star (38 in.), Golden West (center right), Crimson Pirate (30 in.).

Winnetka (22 to 24 in.), mid-season.

Soft Whisper (28 to 30 in.), mid-season.

Newly purchased plants or divisions of your established clumps should be planted 1 foot apart. Dig holes to a depth of 10 to 12 inches, then center a mound of earth in each hole. Set in all plants at depth at which they formerly grew, spreading roots over mound. Fill in with soil; water well.

Hemerocallis may be set into the garden in either spring or fall, and are subject to virtually no disease. They flower most in sun, although they perform adequately in shady locations as well.

Daylilies are actually very undemanding about the soil in which they grow, but will benefit from fertilizing, either in fall or early spring. Mulch the planting bed to hinder weed growth.

Recommended long-time favorites in the mid-season class—and therefore less costly—include Evelyn Claar (33 in., pink); Kindly Light (30 in., citrous yellow); Hesperus (42 in., chrome yellow); Mabel Fuller (38 in., cardinal red); The Doctor (36 in., deep red); and Stars Over Dallas (34 in., pale yellow).

13

PERENNIAL FAVORITES
Hardy Lilies

Over recent decades, hybridizers of hardy lilies have worked magic to give us bulbs that will perform handsomely and, if planted where drainage is good and the site mostly sunny, offer few problems of maintenance or disease control. Select lilies by flowering time to have some in bloom all summer. Imperial Gold, above, is one of the June-July bloomers.

Old-fashioned favorites, tiger lilies bloom in July-August.

July-August bloomer Imperial Crimson.

Joan Evans (orange) and Destiny (yellow) flower in June-July.

15

Chrysanthemums

Gardeners everywhere are indebted to the Chinese and Japanese who have grown and hybridized the chrysanthemum for thousands of years. The spectacular mum shown above is Potomac, an unusual single, two-foot plant with a 5- to 7-inch bloom. Choose varieties grown locally for gardens of the North where deep frost comes early. Or, try growing in pots sunken in the garden, to be brought indoors to bloom in a sunny window prior to killing frost. The best practice for cold regions is to select cold-hardy and early blooming varieties to avoid having hard frost kill off budded chrysanthemums before they unfurl. Look to early blooming cushion-type mums for September flowering, well ahead of expected freeze dates in most areas.

Tantalizer, spider, bears 12-in. flowers; Yellow Arcadia, pompon, with 2-in. bloom.

Powder Puff, yellow anemone, flowers to 5 in.; Deanna Lee, pompon, 3½-in. bloom.

1 In spring, when the new growth is 3 inches tall, dig the plant and pull apart. Select sturdy rooted shoots to transplant to newly prepared fertile soil in sun.

2 When transplanting, shoots should be spaced 1 foot apart. Cut or pinch ¾ inch off top of each newly planted division. When a plant is six inches tall, prune again. In the North, last pruning is July 15. This keeps plants shorter and denser.

3 For bushy, heavily budded plants, every 10 days use a light feeding of balanced plant fertilizer, either liquid or dry, and well watered in. Use mulch of grass clippings, shredded bark, or compost applied 2 inches thick to keep roots cool and conserve ground moisture.

17

Wildflowers

Gardeners who cultivate wildflowers help to preserve our American heritage of natural beauty. Many a wood has been robbed by thoughtless passers-by who plucked or pulled up wildflowers by the roots. But today, almost every garden magazine lists plantsmen who specialize in cultivating wildflowers. Order plants suited to the shady or partly shady spots you can offer, or grow from seed.

Bloodroot (Sanguinaria canadensis), one of spring's early charmers, thrives in part-shade.

Jack-in-the-pulpit (Arisaema triphyllum) shoots up in late spring in shady, moist areas. The plants multiply rather slowly; and produce red berries in late summer.

Hepatica, its blue flowers at center of planting, above, is named for its liver-shaped leaves. Here it's hidden by the foliage of Dutchman's breeches, pink-flowered neighbors. Both need shade.

Marsh marigold, when given the very moist location it needs, rewards you with a yearly springtime show of glossy gold bloom. Difficult to grow from seed; best started from purchased plants.

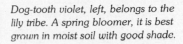

Dog-tooth violet, left, belongs to the lily tribe. A spring bloomer, it is best grown in moist soil with good shade.

Trillium, below, needs moisture and shade. This showy variety (Trillium grandiflorum) will increase yearly.

Virginia bluebells (Mertensia virginica) bloom a bit later in spring than most other wildflowers pictured. They flower in sun or shade, and spread rapidly. Fine companion to spring bulbs.

Shooting-star (Dodecatheon) gets its name from its cyclamen-like bloom. Give this spring bloomer good drainage in a shady or part-shady location in moderately rich soil that's not too dry.

19

WILDFLOWERS

Name	Description	Light and Soil	Propagation	Special Helps
Alumroot (heuchera)	Tiny blossoms on stems 16 to 36 in. tall; May to August	Shade Well-drained, dry soil	Seeds Division	Leaves mottled when young
Anemone, rue (anemonella)	Early blossoms on stems 5 to 9 in. tall; white and pink from March to June	Shade Well-drained, dry soil	Seeds Division	Divide after plant has died back in the fall
Arbutus, trailing (epigaea)	Tubular blossoms on 3-in. plants; white and pink with white berries, March to May	Partial shade Well-drained, dry soil	Seeds Stem cuttings Stem layering	Keep well-mulched
Baneberry (actaea)	Small white blossoms on 24-in. plants; red or white berries in April and May	Shade Well-drained, dry soil	Seeds Division	Sow seeds in the fall
Bellwort (uvularia)	Yellow blossoms on graceful 4- to 12-in. plants, April to June	Shade Well-drained, moist soil	Seeds Division	Fleshy winged seed capsules
Bishop's-cap (mitella)	Tiny white flowers on 6- to 12-in. plants from April to June	Shade Well-drained, moist soil	Seeds Division	Keep well-mulched
Black-eyed susan (rudbeckia)	Flat, daisy-like flowers on 2-ft. wiry stems; July and August	Sun Well-drained soil	Seeds Often self-sows	Often grown as a biennial
Bloodroot (sanguinaria)	Large-leaved plants 8 to 10 in. high; single white flowers in April and May	Shade Well-drained, dry soil	Seeds Division	Multiplies rapidly; forms thick mat
Bluebells (mertensia)	Tall 2-ft. stems of blue flowers on 12- to 15-in. plants in April and May	Sun or partial shade Well-drained, moist soil	Seeds Division	Plants disappear during the summer
Butterfly weed (asclepias)	Clusters of red-orange flowers on 2-ft. plants; July and August	Sun Well-drained, dry soil	Seeds Root cuttings	Brilliant color
Cinquefoil (potentilla)	Tiny white flowers on 3- to 6-in. plants that turn red in the fall; June to August	Shade Well-drained, dry, acid soil	Seeds Division Stem cuttings	Good ground cover
Columbine, wild (aquilegia)	Finely cut, pendulous flowers on 1- to 2-ft. plants from April through July; yellow and red	Shade Well-drained, dry, slightly acid soil	Seeds Often self-sows	Very showy
Coneflower, prairie (ratibida)	Large yellow flowers on plants up to 6 ft. tall from June to August	Sun Well-drained, dry soil	Seeds Division	Graceful and showy
Coneflower, purple (echinacea)	Large, single purple flowers on plants 3- to 4 ft. tall from June to October	Sun Well-drained, dry soil	Seeds Division	Tall and impressive

Name	Description	Light and Soil	Propagation	Special Helps
Crowfoot, buttercup (ranunculus)	Small yellow flowers on plants 6 to 24 in. tall from April to August	Shade or partial shade Tolerant of most soil types	Seeds Division	Can become pestiferous
Dog-tooth violet (erythronium)	Solitary white flowers on plants 6 in. tall in April and May	Shade Well-drained, moist soil	Offsets Seeds	Forms a dense mat; leaves are mottled with brown
Dutchman's-breeches (dicentra)	Unusually shaped white flowers clustered on stems from plants 6 to 12 in. high, April to May	Shade Well-drained, dry soil	Division Seeds	Disappears after flowering
Evening primrose (oenothera)	Pale yellow fragrant flowers on plants 2 to 4 ft. tall in July and August	Sun Well-drained, dry soil	Seeds	Flowers open only at night Treat as a biennial
Flag, blue (iris)	Large, purple blossoms on plants 2 to 3 ft. tall in May and June	Sun Moist-to-wet, slightly acid soil	Division Seeds Often self-sows	Forms a dense colony
Foamflower, False miterwort (tiarella)	Small white flowers clustered on stems from plants 6 to 12 in. tall	Shade Well-drained, moist soil	Division Seeds	Effective in mass
Forget-me-not (myosotis)	Pale blue flowers with yellow centers on 6-in. plants all summer long	Sun Well-drained, moist-to-wet soil	Division Seeds	Keep very moist
Gentian, closed, blue (gentiana)	Tubular violet flowers on plants 1 ft. tall in August and September	Sun or partial shade Well-drained, moist-to-wet, slightly acid soil	Division Seeds	Flowers remain closed
Geranium, wild (geranium)	Large, red-violet flowers in clusters on plants 24 in. tall	Shade Well-drained, moist soil	Division Seeds	Effective in mass
Ginger, wild (asarum)	Inconspicuous tubular violet-brown flowers at the base of plants 4 to 8 in. tall in April and May	Shade Well-drained, moist soil	Division Rhizome cuttings	Interesting ground cover
Hepaticas (hepatica)	Showy rose, white, or blue flowers on short 6-in. plants from April to May	Shade Well-drained, dry, slightly acid soil	Division Seeds Often self-sows	Valued for early color
Jack-in-the-pulpit (arisaema)	Unusual vase-shaped greenish-brown flowers on plants 2 ft. tall from April to June. Red berries follow later in the season	Shade Well-drained, moist soil	Seeds Often self-sows	Very showy and attractive
Jacob's-ladder (polemonium)	Small clusters of blue flowers on 3-ft. plants in June and July	Shade Well-drained, moist soil	Seeds Division	Fine border plant
Lady's-slipper, yellow (cypripedium)	Very showy yellow flowers, often veined in blue, on plants to 30-in. tall in May	Shade Well-drained, moist soil	Division	Give an annual top dressing of compost

WILDFLOWERS

Name	Description	Light and Soil	Propagation	Special Helps
Lobelia, blue (lobelia)	Tiny blue flowers on plants 2 to 3 ft. tall from August to October	Sun or partial shade Well-drained, moist soil	Offsets Division Stem cuttings Seeds	Valuable for late-summer color
Mallow rose (hibiscus)	Large red, pink, or white flowers on plants 6 ft. tall from July to September	Sun Well-drained, moist soil	Division Stem cuttings Seeds	Use as a background plant
Marigold, marsh (caltha)	Brilliant yellow flowers in small clusters on plants 2 ft. tall in April and May	Sun Moist-to-wet soil	Division	Plants disappear in summer
Mayapple, mandrake (podophyllum)	Single white daisy-like flower on 12- to 18-in. plants in April and May Unusual umbrella-like leaves; 12- to 18-in. bears yellow fruit in August	Partial to full shade Well-drained, moist soil	Division Seeds	Rapid spreader Good, quick ground cover
Meadow rue, early (thalictrum)	Inconspicuous greenish-violet flowers on 2-ft. plants in April and May	Shade Well-drained, moist soil	Division Seeds	Handsome, dainty foliage
Meadow rue, tall (thalictrum)	Large clusters of white flowers on plants to 10 ft. tall from August to September	Sun Well-drained, moist-to-wet soil	Seeds Division Stem cuttings	Use as a background plant
Partridgeberry (mitchella)	Small white flowers on plants to 6 in. tall in June and July Small red berries follow later in the season	Shade Well-drained, moist, acid soil	Stem cuttings Seeds	Effective ground cover
Pasqueflower (anemone)	Large showy, purple flowers on 16-in. plants in March and April	Sun Well-drained, dry soil	Seeds Root cuttings	Very early and attractive
Phlox, blue (phlox)	Pale blue flowers on 6- to 15-in. stems in April and May The nonflowering part hugs the ground	Partial shade Well-drained, dry soil	Division Stem cuttings	Often form large clumps
Phlox, downy (phlox)	Red-violet flowers on stems from 6 to 15 in. tall in May and June The nonflowering part hugs the ground	Partial shade Well-drained, dry soil	Division Stem cuttings	Plant in sandy soil
Poppy, California (eschscholzia)	Brilliant orange cup-like flowers on plants 10 to 20 in. tall from April to June	Sun Well-drained, dry soil	Seeds	Vigorous and hardy
Prairie rose (rosa)	Handsome pink flowers in small clusters on spreading branches up to 15 ft. long from May to July	Sun Well-drained, dry soil	Seeds Stem layering	Branches are thornless

Name	Description	Light and Soil	Propagation	Special Helps
Sand verbena (abronia)	Small pink, yellow, or lilac flowers on 12-in. plants from May to September	Sun Well-drained, dry soil	Seeds	Trailing stems
Shooting-star (dodecatheon)	Small, attractive red-violet flowers in clusters on 1 ft. stalks in May and June	Light shade Well-drained, moist soil	Division Seeds Root cuttings	Plant disappears in summer
Snakeroot (cimicifuga)	Tiny white blossoms in spike clusters on plants 8 ft. tall from July to September	Shade Well-drained, moist soil	Division Seeds	Use as a background plant
Solomon's-seal (polygonatum)	Inconspicuous greenish-white, bell-shaped flowers appear under the leaves on plants 1 to 2 ft. tall in May and June Bluish-black berries follow later in the season	Shade Well-drained, dry, slightly acid soil	Seeds	Interesting leaf arrangement Good ground cover in shady areas
Spiderwort (tradescantia)	Blue or white flowers in small terminal clusters on 1- to 2-ft. grass-like plants from June to August	Sun or partial shade Well-drained, moist soil	Division Seeds Stem cuttings	Vigorous and quick-growing
Spring-beauty (claytonia)	Delicate pinkish-white blossoms on plants 4 to 6 in. tall from March to May	Shade Well-drained, dry soil	Division Seeds Often self-sows	Good ground cover in shady areas
Sunflower, sawtooth (helianthus)	Large yellow blossoms with brown centers in clusters on plants 10 in. tall from July to October	Sun Well-drained soil	Seeds Division	Showy background plant
Toothwort (dentaria)	Tiny pinkish-white flowers in small terminal clusters on plants 6 to 12 in. tall in April and May	Shade Well-drained, moist soil	Seeds Division	Valued for early spring color
Trillium (trillium)	Showy white or purple blossom on erect terminal stems on 12-in. plants from April to June	Shade Well-drained, moist soil	Seeds Division	Effective in mass
Turtlehead (chelone)	White or pink terminal flowers on plants 3 ft. tall from July to September	Shade Well-drained, moist soil	Seeds Division Stem cuttings Often self-sows	Interesting and handsome
Violet, blue (viola)	Blue flowers on small 6- to 8-in. plants from April to June	Partial to full shade Well-drained, moist soil	Seeds Division Often self-sows	Can become pestiferous
Wood aster, blue (aster)	Small, light purple flowers in open clusters on plants 4 ft. tall in August and September	Partial to full shade Well-drained, moist soil	Division	Good background plants

Ornamental Grasses

Seldom-used ornamental grasses deserve your attention as dramatic landscape accents. For greatest effect, clump two or more plants of one species near a similar group of another. Repeat these clumps at intervals for a balanced display. The dramatic grouping at the edge of a patio, below, is just one of the shows ornamental grasses can make. Three varieties are effectively teamed: at the back, tall *Spartina michauxiana* or cord-grass; in the center is tasseled annual fountain grass or *Pennisetum ruppeli;* and around the edges of the patio are tufts of *Festuca glauca* or blue fescue.

Another tall perennial ornamental worthy of consideration is *Erianthus ravennae* or plume grass; it sends up 12-foot plumes from 3-foot plants. Bamboo-like *Arundo donax,* 6 to 8 feet tall, is hardy in the South and makes a good potted plant in the North if you've a suitable spot to overwinter it indoors.

A popular edging plant with glossy foliage, liriope, above, blooms in summer, its flowers resembling grape hyacinth. Zone 5.

Blue fescue forms 10-inch clumps in sun or shade. Zone 3.

Another ornamental grass which is highly decorative is *Miscanthus sinensis,* a winter-hardy perennial that will grow as tall as 6 feet high. A variegated form of this species which is related to zebra grass is also available.

Carex morrowi variegata has white stripes on green leaves and is just 1 foot tall. In the entry planting, pictured at right, ornamental grass, *Helictotrichon sempervirens,* has been set into a bed of spring heath. Its distinctive, arching foliage and unusual color make it an excellent accent plant for the use illustrated, or for front-of-the-border placement in other garden locations.

Helictotrichon sempervirens, a member of the oats family, lends distinction to an entry planting in a bed of heath.

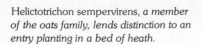

25

Biennials

The renowned, late horticulturist, Liberty Hyde Bailey, defined biennials as "plants that bloom a year after seeds are sown, then make seeds and die." But there are confusing factors about such well-known biennials as foxglove, honesty, and hollyhock: they self-sow or multiply by off-shoots, often seeming to be perennial.

The best way to grow biennials from seed, except in warmer zones, is to plant seed outdoors in early August, transplanting to a cold frame before frost. Set plants into garden in May.

Double hollyhocks, like their single cousins, need full sun.

ALPINE FORGET-ME-NOT

Myosotis alpestris, grown as a low (1-foot) carpet of sky-blue under the brilliant spring-flowering bulbs, creates an unforgettable sight.

This plant prefers moist soil and a half-shaded location. It has little tolerance for the hot weather of summer, and goes to seed when that season arrives.

Left undisturbed for a time, it sends up seedling plants which you can transfer to a cold frame or protected area for plants to set into your border next spring. Transplant to border as soon as the ground can be worked.

If you live where springs tend to be long and cool, you can wait for the ground to thaw, plant seed outdoors, and have bloom within 6 weeks.

CANTERBURY BELLS

Campanula medium, blooming in early summer, could be the star of the mixed flower border.

On 2-foot stems, single cups may measure as much as 3 inches in depth, framed by "saucers" 3 to 4 inches across.

This plant is available in both single and double forms, and in shades of blue, rose, and white. Use it to best advantage in a middle-of-the-border location.

Sow seed of this biennial in August; transplant to a cold frame for the winter, and set out in spring when all danger of frost has passed.

ENGLISH DAISY

Bellis perennis, opposite bottom, is aster-like in appearance, endearing for prolific bloom in the spring on 4- to 6-inch plants.

Perfect for front-of-border placement, it requires moist soil and grows best in part-shade. Flower colors vary from pink to deep rose.

FOXGLOVE

Digitalis purpurea, opposite above, is one of the graceful verticals that are so effective in combination with plants of more bushy growth habit. Most varieties are from 4 to 6 feet tall, although one variety, Foxy, forms a bushy plant of only 3 feet in height at maturity. Seed for foxglove is commonly sold in a mixture that includes white, cream, yellow, rose, red, and lavender. The Giant Rusty variety, however, produces all rusty-red flowers with bearded lips. Six feet tall, it needs staking. All foxglove varieties bloom in June or early July, in sun or part-shade.

HOLLYHOCK

Alcea rosea so readily seeds itself that many take it for a true perennial, and it is sometimes so listed in seed catalogs. In a clump against a garden wall or fence, hollyhocks make a fine sight. They need full sun to make strong stems, and even then, tall types (6 to 8 feet) will often require staking.

Or, use hollyhocks as a back-of-the-border plant. From July onward, you will enjoy single or double blooms in pink, white, red, yellow, and lavender shades.

HONESTY

Lunaria annua, also known as the money plant, is grown largely for its charm as a dried flower, lending the shining silver glow of its 2-inch round seed pods to winter bouquets.

Plants grow from 1½ to 3 feet tall. This biennial is so apt to reseed itself that, in most climates, the main chore may be to pull the unwanted seedlings each spring.

PANSY

Viola tricolor, for all its charming pansy "faces," may not be worth the effort it takes to grow from seed if your area is apt to have springs that are short and often abruptly ended by a spell of hot, dry weather.

Then, buy young plants and set out as early in spring as you dare; plant near spring flowering bulbs in a moist, part-shade location.

SWEET WILLIAM

Dianthus barbatus is another self-sower of great vigor and, in most years, will behave like a perennial. Blooming in May and June on 12- to 20-inch stems (or 5 to 6 inches for the newer dwarfs), they're popular both for their color and fragrance in borders. Roundabout (mixed reds, roses, and pinks) and Wee Willie (red) are both 4-inch dwarfs. Plant in a sunny, well-drained garden location.

Graceful, tall foxglove, above, and low-growing English daisy, below, are rewarding biennials. Alternate clumps of English daisies and pansies for an effective early spring border.

ABCs
of
Perennials

When you plant perennials, you plant for long-lasting beauty. And you hope for minimal care on your part. To achieve these two desirable—and reasonable—goals, make plans before you plant. With perennials, if you've planned and planted well, you can expect to sit back and admire the results of your efforts for years to come.

But planning and planting techniques are all-important, and it is to this section that you should look for vital facts on season of bloom, zonal hardiness (see also pages 92 and 93), height of plant at maturity, preferences as to sun or shade, soil type, color or colors available, and special cultural information. So, whether you're a new or an experienced garden hand, check this section before you decide whether and where to add a new member to your garden.

Oriental poppies are available in a wide range of colors.

A

ACHILLEA
see yarrow

ACONITUM
see monkshood

ADONIS
(Adonis vernalis); also called spring adonis

ZONE: 3   HEIGHT: 12 inches
FLOWER COLOR: yellow
BLOOM TIME: March-April
LIGHT: sun or light shade
PROPAGATION: seed or root division

Blooming early, along with snow-drops, adonis has solitary, terminal flowers on leafy stems. Foliage is narrow and very finely cut.

Culture is easy in any average soil, though the plant prefers moist woodsy earth. Use adonis at the front of a mixed perennial border that includes spring-flowering bulbs, or plant in a rock garden.

Grow new plants from seed in summer or divide and replant established clumps in late spring, summer, or fall.

AGERATUM
(Eupatorium coelestinum); also called hardy ageratum

ZONE: 3   HEIGHT: 2 feet
FLOWER COLOR: blue
BLOOM TIME: August-September
LIGHT: part-shade
PROPAGATION: root division

Also called mist flower, this hardy perennial is a valuable addition to mixed borders in need of late summer color—especially in the blue range. It takes its common name from annual ageratum, which is not a relative, although they do bear some similarities, especially in color of bloom.

No special culture is needed for this easy-to-grow plant, but it is at its best in light shade.

Reproduces readily in the form of spreading clumps. Spring is the best time to lift, divide, and replant.

ALYSSUM
(Aurinia saxatilis); also called basket-of-gold

ZONE: 3   HEIGHT: 12 to 15 inches
FLOWER COLOR: yellow
BLOOM TIME: early spring
LIGHT: sun or part-sun
PROPAGATION: seed, stem cuttings, or root division

Ordinary garden soil suits this hardy perennial, which flowers most prolifically in full sun.

A. saxatilis 'citrina' is the most

floriferous variety; *A. saxatilis 'compacta'* has similar growth habits but is somewhat shorter.

Note that this is *not* the plant referred to as "sweet alyssum," which is an annual of wide usage, a dwarf in habit, and available in white, blues, pinks, and purples.

ALKANET
see anchusa

ANCHUSA
(Anchusa azurea); also called alkanet

ZONE: 3   HEIGHT: 1 to 4 feet
FLOWER COLOR: blue
BLOOM TIME: June onward
LIGHT: sun or part-sun
PROPAGATION: root division in spring or fall

Depending upon the variety you pick, this perennial forget-me-not grows up to 4 feet tall (*Anchusa azurea,* Dropmore variety), or only 12 inches (Little John).

Bright blue flowers on plants of pyramidal form with somewhat rough or hairy foliage are characteristic of all varieties.

If spent bloom is regularly cut (not allowed to go to seed), this plant will often continue to bloom into September. Clumps multiply at a slow rate. If more rapid increase is wanted, allow plants to go to seed.

ANTHEMIS
(Anthemis tinctoria); also called golden marguerite

ZONE: 3   HEIGHT: 30 to 36 inches
FLOWER COLOR: yellow
BLOOM TIME: June to frost
LIGHT: sun or part-shade
PROPAGATION: root division

Any garden soil seems to suit this long-flowering perennial. Two-inch-wide blooms of a deep yellow appear on plants which may grow as tall as 3 feet under ideal conditions. Generous with its bloom, it's good as a mid-border plant, allowing you to cut long-lasting bouquets during all summer months. Divide established clumps to start new plants.

AQUILEGIA
see columbine

ARMERIA
see thrift

ARTEMISIA
(Artemisia sp.); also called wormwood

ZONE: 3   HEIGHT: 6 inches
FLOWER COLOR: silver-gray foliage
BLOOM TIME: spring through summer
LIGHT: sun, part-shade
PROPAGATION: cuttings or root division

Silver Mound, *Artemesia schmidtiana,* is the most widely known of cultivated artemisias. Its cool, ferny foliage contrasts well with the green leaves and the colorful bloom of other plants in a mixed perennial border. Use it as a transition plant between bloom colors that could clash if set next to each other. It's a good rock garden plant as well, with mounds spreading out to as much as a foot in width.

If mid-season heat makes it look ragged, cut back sharply. It will soon put up fresh growth.

Another favorite, *A. stellerana,* grows 2 feet tall, and is called dusty miller or old woman, having the same trait of white-looking foliage as does Silver Mound. It, too, is useful in borders, though at mid- rather than front-of-the-border locations. Thrives in almost any type of garden soil.

A. abotanum, called old man or southernwood, reaches 2 to 3 feet tall with fragrant, gray foliage and small yellow flowers in August.

Silver King artemisia (*A. albula*) has silvery gray leaves and can reach a height of 3½ feet.

Propagate the shrubby artemisias such as Silver Mound by rooting stem cuttings in a cold frame in autumn. For herbaceous artemisias on which stems die back in the fall, such as Silver King, increase by root division in late fall or early spring.

As with many common names, a certain amount of confusion exists here, also. Some seed catalogs list a perennial cineraria as "dusty miller" in both dwarf and taller varieties. These have the silver-white foliage that is typical of the artemesias discussed above, and they may be put to similar uses.

ASCLEPIAS
see butterfly weed

ASTER
(Aster sp.); also called michaelmas daisy

ZONE: 4   HEIGHT: to 48 inches
FLOWER COLOR: pinks, blues, purples
BLOOM TIME: most kinds bloom late summer-fall
LIGHT: sun or part-shade
PROPAGATION: root division in spring or fall

Hardy asters demand no more than adequate sun and water to supply you with important late bloom—mostly in August and September. Among the best-loved of the many varieties available are:

Harrington's Pink, Sailor Boy (violet flowers with yellow eyes), and Boningale White (double, with yellow eyes).

There are other hardy asters that do not bloom at such tall heights, and a few that bloom all summer. Best of this last named group is *Aster frikarti,* which does bloom from June to frost, with flowers of lavender-blue, and stems from 24 to 30 inches tall.

Among the dwarfs of the tribe—plants that grow 8 to 15 inches tall—are Jenny—15 inches, cyclamen-red bloom—and Romany—6 to 8 inches tall, with violet flowers from early September until frost.

Tall-growing varieties should be lifted, divided, and replanted about every three years. As with chrysanthemums, throw out woody center portions of plants, divide healthy parts, and re-set about a foot apart. Clumps spread quite rapidly, but new plants do not come true from seed.

If you pinch tops back sharply in June, tallest varieties can be kept somewhat shorter. Left unpinched, tallest varieties will probably have to be staked in August.

ASTILBE
(Astilbea arendsi);
also called false spirea

ZONE: 4 **HEIGHT:** 15 to 30 inches
FLOWER COLOR: pink, red, white, salmon
BLOOM TIME: June-July
LIGHT: sun-shade
PROPAGATION: root division in spring or fall

This handsome plant supplies the answer to a question that plagues many gardeners who want color in shade. Although it will perform in sun, it much prefers shade, and puts up big, feathery plumes of bloom above neatly formed dark green fern-like leaves.

Astilbes prefer a damp location, but will perform adequately in almost any soil. They're hardy enough to use as ground cover in shady spots, and will bring welcome color to mid-border locations in mixed perennial gardens.

If summers are long and hot in the zone where you live, be sure to mulch around base of astilbes to retain needed ground moisture.

B

BABY'S-BREATH
(Gypsophila paniculata)

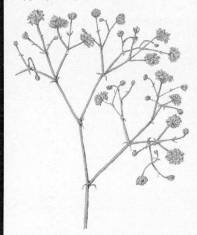

ZONE: 3 **HEIGHT:** 4 feet
FLOWER COLOR: white, pink
BLOOM TIME: June-July
LIGHT: full sun
PROPAGATION: root cuttings in midsummer

Perennial baby's-breath needs well-drained alkaline soil, full sun, and lots of space if it is to be at its best. Because plants grow almost as wide as they are tall, set new plants about 6 feet apart in the location where you'll want them permanently. They send down a tap root that makes it virtually impossible to move big plants with success.

Because they are so tall, with rather weak stems, they'll need to be well staked so wind and rain won't send them sprawling over their neighbors in the perennial border.

But they are worth the trouble—as a source for cut and dried flowers, as well as for their feathery charm in the border itself.

Well-loved varieties include Bristol Fairy (white) and Pink Fairy. Both are doubles.

There is a creeping variety of the plant, *Gypsophila repens* (either white or pink) that grows only a few inches tall and is best suited to rockeries.

BALLOON FLOWER
(Platycodon grandiflorus)

ZONE: 3 **HEIGHT:** 20 inches
FLOWER COLOR: blue, pink, white
BLOOM TIME: July-August
LIGHT: sun
PROPAGATION: sow seed in spring or summer, or buy root starts

Most popular in its blue form, this hardy perennial takes a year or two to become well established, then goes on to bloom for years. It gets its common name from the fact that buds are round and puffy before they open, resembling tiny balloons. The fleshy, tuber-like roots should be planted so crowns are just below the soil level, with at least 1 foot

ZONE: 3 HEIGHT: 4 to 5 feet
FLOWER COLOR: deep blue
BLOOM TIME: June
LIGHT: sun or part-shade
PROPAGATION: seed or root division

Native to North America, baptisia is a very hardy perennial, able to withstand drought. Although it will grow in full sun, it prefers some shade. Flowers resemble those of the pea family but are of an intense, dark blue. If pods are left on the plant, wild birds will eat seeds during the winter months.

This plant is ideal for sloping banks, but is not without problems in a perennial border, since it grows rankly, once established, and may need staking while in bloom. *Baptisia australis* (blue) is best suited to perennial gardens. *B. tinctoria*, which has yellow flowers, often is grown in wild gardens. *B. alba* is one of several white species.

Variety Cambridge Scarlet puts out brilliant bloom from late June on into September, and is attractive when planted close to yellow daylilies.

BELLFLOWER
see campanula

BELLIS
(Bellis perennis); also known as English daisy

between plants. Don't try to move them once they're planted.

It is not difficult to grow this plant from seed. Start seed in late summer when nights begin to be cool. Transplant to a cold frame for the winter, then move into garden after all frost danger has passed.

BAPTISIA
(Baptisia australis); also known as blue or false indigo

BASKET-OF-GOLD
see alyssum

BEE-BALM
(Monarda didyma); also known as bergamot

ZONE: 4 HEIGHT: 2 to 3 feet
FLOWER COLOR: pink, red, purple, white
BLOOM TIME: July-August
LIGHT: sun or part-shade
PROPAGATION: root division

Bee-balm is indeed attractive to bees as well as to hummingbirds.

Valuable as a mid-border plant, it is extremely hardy and withstands drought. Even when not in bloom, it's easily recognized from its square stem. Not at all fussy as to soil, bee-balm will perform well even in fairly sandy or heavy soil, though it does best in a lighter loam. Clumps increase rather rapidly, and more plants may be had by lifting, dividing, and replanting divisions in early spring.

ZONE: 3 HEIGHT: 6 to 8 inches
FLOWER COLOR: pink, white, red
BLOOM TIME: spring
LIGHT: part-shade
PROPAGATION: seed or root division

These dainty plants make attractive companions to spring-flowering bulbs, but resent long, hot, dry summers, under which conditions they behave as biennials rather than perennials. If pansies do well for you, so will English daisies.

To grow from seed, sow in late summer or early autumn in a protected location or cold frame, then transplant into flower border or bed as early as the ground can be worked. Space the plants 5 inches apart, and if growing conditions are suitable, they will self-sow generously.

BLEEDINGHEART
(Dicentra spectabilis)

ZONE: 4   **HEIGHT:** 24 inches
FLOWER COLOR: pink
BLOOM TIME: early spring
LIGHT: part-shade
PROPAGATION: cuttings or root division

This old-fashioned favorite has lacy foliage, and sends up racemes loaded with gracefully drooping pink, heart-shaped flowers. Plant about 24 inches apart, as the clump will gradually increase in size.

When set close to flowering bulbs and either annual or perennial (anchusa) forget-me-nots, bleedingheart has endearing charm in the spring garden.

As summer progresses, foliage is prone to die back. For this reason, it's wise to mark location with a stake to avoid disturbing the root if you plan to overplant bulb areas with annuals for summer color.

In recent years, some shorter varieties of bleedingheart have been introduced and described in plant catalogs as "blooming all summer." These, however, are not as reliably hardy as *Dicentra spectabilis* described above, nor do they tolerate heat well.

BLUE FALSE INDIGO
see baptisia

BLUE MARGUERITE
see felicia

BRUNNERA
(Brunnera macrophylla); also known as Siberian forget-me-not and Siberian bugloss

ZONE: 4   **HEIGHT:** 18 inches
FLOWER COLOR: blue
BLOOM TIME: May
LIGHT: part-shade
PROPAGATION: seed or root cuttings

Sometimes listed as *Anchusa myosotidiflora,* brunnera should be thought of as a half-hardy perennial. The bloom closely resembles that of the perennial forget-me-not, *A. azurea,* but it appears earlier, and

therefore has value as a complement to the spring flowering bulbs. May be grown from seed sown in late summer, then transplanted into the border as early as the soil can be worked.

In fact, it's wise to allow some bloom to go to seed, saving it in case the mother plant fails to emerge after a fall and winter of adverse weather conditions. Seed also may be sown indoors in early spring (March-April), but young plants are unlikely to bloom that same spring.

BUGLOSS
see brunnera

BUTTERCUPS
(Ranunculus sp.)

ZONE: 4   **HEIGHT:** 18 inches
FLOWER COLOR: yellow
BLOOM TIME: May
LIGHT: sun or part-shade
PROPAGATION: seed or root division

An enormous family, the buttercups include many wildflowers. One that's particularly

33

worth growing in the mixed perennial garden is *Ranunculus acris.* It has double shiny yellow flowers on stems from 12 to 18 inches tall, with attractive, deeply cut leaves.

Acris is a creeper and sends out a large number of runners each spring. But these are not difficult to control if you simply pull them off before they take root. Their yellow flowers are a pleasant contrast to the blues and purples of bearded iris, with which their season of bloom coincides.

R. amplexicaulis, 10 to 12 inches high, is a good candidate for the rock garden.

BUTTERFLY WEED
(*Asclepias tuberosa*)

ZONE: 4   **HEIGHT:** 2 to 3 feet
FLOWER COLOR: orange
BLOOM TIME: summer
LIGHT: sun
PROPAGATION: seed or division

Butterflies are attracted to the umbels of brilliant orange bloom on this hardy perennial. Flowering from July to September, it fills a gap in the mixed perennial border season of bloom and is most welcome.

Not fussy about soil, this plant must have good drainage and sun if it is to perform at its best.

It makes its greatest effect when set out in groups of three or more. Try to plant where you'll want permanent growth, as large plants are very difficult to move.

Seemingly unaffected by any plant disease, butterfly weed is handsome in bouquets of cut flowers and is long-lasting. But as it's slow to come up in spring, clumps should be marked to avoid damage when cultivating or planting at that season of the year.

C

CAMPANULA
(*Campanula* sp.); also known as bellflower

ZONE: 3   **HEIGHT:** 8 to 36 inches
FLOWER COLOR: blue, white
BLOOM TIME: June
LIGHT: sun, light shade
PROPAGATION: root division in early spring

There are so many attractive members of this family—some hardy all the way from zone 3 southward, others not hardy farther north than zone 5—that it is difficult to choose any one or two as "best."

Campanula carpatica makes an excellent edging plant, sends up blue bloom all summer, and is hardy zone 3 southward. Its relative, *C. carpatica alba,* has the same growth habits but bears white flowers.

C. glomerata has both blue and white varieties that grow 18 to 20 inches tall, bloom throughout June and July, and are ideal mixed border plants. They multiply generously in zone 4 southward.

C. persicifolia, or peach-bells, has white or blue nodding flowers up to 1½ inches long on 3-foot stems. Some varieties that are July flowering include doubles. Set plants of this variety 10 to 12 inches apart. Zone 3.

C. lactiflora varieties are generally not hardy north of zone 5. They are part-shade tolerant, and colors are mostly in the blue range.

All campanula should have winter protection; plants should be lifted,

divided, and replanted every two or three years to ensure hardiness. Do this after the bloom period ends.

All require moderately rich, well-drained soil. Since none is easily grown from seed, it is advisable to start with young plants, set out in spring.

C. medium, a member of this family commonly called Canterbury-bells, is a biennial rather than a perennial and is covered on page 26.

CANDYTUFT
(*Iberis sempervirens*)

ZONE: 3   **HEIGHT:** 4 to 8 inches
FLOWER COLOR: white
BLOOM TIME: May
LIGHT: sun
PROPAGATION: seed, stem cuttings, or division

Perennial candytuft has foliage that stays evergreen in mild climates; it dies down where winters are severe. Cut the tips back an inch or two right after the blooming season.

Use candytuft as an edging, as a companion to May-flowering tulips, or in rock gardens. Plants require a rich, well-drained garden soil. If your soil is poor, improve it by adding generous amounts of compost; if there is too much clay, incorporate coarse sand and fine pebbles with compost.

One variety, Autumn Snow, blooms again in September, after having bloomed in May, then stays in bloom until frost. It's 7 inches tall.

Variety Pygmy grows only 4 inches tall, and is easily propagated by division. Or, use cuttings taken in the spring, rooted in vermiculite, and then planted. Makes a good underplanting to May tulips.

CANTERBURY-BELLS
see campanula

CARDINAL FLOWER
see lobelia

CATANANCHE
see cupid's-dart

CATCHFLY
see lychnis

CENTAUREA
(Centaurea montana) also known as mountain bluet, cornflower, or perennial bachelor's button

ZONE: 4 **HEIGHT:** 2 feet
FLOWER COLOR: blue, yellow
BLOOM TIME: June-July
LIGHT: sun, part-sun
PROPAGATION: root division or seed

Most members of the centaurea family are annuals, including *Centaurea cyanus,* also called bachelor's button.

C. montana is one of the perennials with silvery leaves and blue bloom measuring up to 3 inches across. The variety *C. montana citrina* has similar growth habits, but blooms are lemon-yellow in color.

None is fussy about soil, though good drainage is important. Use them in a mixed border for mid-season color and for cut flowers.

To propagate from seed, sow in late summer, when nights are cool, then transplant to a cold frame for the winter. Set into border after all frost danger has passed. They will bloom that summer.

CENTRANTHUS
see Jupiter's-beard

CERASTIUM
(Cerastium tomentosum); also known as snow-in-summer

ZONE: 2 **HEIGHT:** 6 inches
FLOWER COLOR: white
BLOOM TIME: summer
LIGHT: sun
PROPAGATION: seed, cuttings, or division

Cerastium can be a pest if planted in a mixed border, as it has the tenacity and the will to reproduce fairly rampantly. But if you have a dry, sunny spot, choose it for a cool, silvery-looking ground cover.

Although it puts forth white flowers in early summer, cerastium is grown more for the foliage than for bloom. It survives in soil that is almost pure sand. Space 10 inches apart as plants spread to 8 inches

each. It's easy to grow from seed sown in late spring in areas where you want growth. It won't bloom the first season, but it will put on a good foliage display and become well established by the second year.

CERATOSTIGMA
see leadwort

CHINESE-LANTERN
(Physalis alkekengi)

ZONE: 3 **HEIGHT:** 2 feet
FLOWER COLOR: bright red "lanterns"
BLOOM TIME: July-August
LIGHT: sun, part-sun
PROPAGATION: seed or root division

Easy to grow from seed, Chinese-lantern plants should be given a bed of their own. They're such pervasive growers that they tend to "take over" and so are undesirable members of a mixed perennial border.

35

The plant is grown almost entirely for its red, hollow, inflated husks which enclose the fruit.

Cut stems when husks are red and keep in a cool, dry place. They make delightful additions to the dried arrangements of autumn.

CHRISTMAS ROSE
see helleborus

CHRYSANTHEMUM
(Chrysanthemum morifolium); also known as hardy chrysanthemum; also see *painted daisy, shasta daisy, and feverfew.*

ZONE: 3-5 **HEIGHT:** 28 inches
FLOWER COLOR: white, yellow, bronze, purple, red
BLOOM TIME: autumn
LIGHT: full sun
PROPAGATION: root division in spring or cuttings

Garden-grown chrysanthemums belong on everyone's "best-loved" group of perennials, not only for their beauty, but also because they bloom so late in the season, when almost every other garden plant has closed its color show for the year.

Time of bloom for most hardy chrysanthemums is determined by day length. As days grow shorter, this particular plant is stimulated to come into bloom. This is why you can buy mums from the florist's greenhouse the year 'round. He can simulate nature's time clock with the use of artificial light and heavy polyethylene to cover plants early, and thus fool them into bloom.

Choose chrysanthemum varieties to match your season. That is, pick those that will bloom before the expected date of first killing frost. Most can take a light frost—where night temperatures dip only slightly below 32° F., then rise rapidly. And you can protect plants on nights when light frost is expected by covering overnight with old sheets or newspapers weighted down so the wind can't carry them off. But don't use plastic bags. Cold easily penetrates them and they will not prevent frost damage.

Major types of chrysanthemums developed over the years by plant hybridizers include:

Cushion chrysanthemums: 12 to 18 inches tall; compact growth with lots of bloom. Good for cutting and for use in the mixed border or in separate beds. Among this group are quite a few early bloomers good for areas where frost arrives early. Almost every color you can think of in the chrysanthemum range is represented by some member of this group.

Decorative chrysanthemums: These plants are taller and less compact in growth habits than are cushion mums. Most will need staking to prevent toppling by strong autumn winds. All are excellent for cut flowers. Bloom dates tend to be in late September. All the usual colors are included in this variety.

Pompon chrysanthemums: Habit of growth is closer to cushion than to decorative mums, but more spreading. The group is excellent for cut flowers, but not as attractive in the mixed border. Grow in a cutting garden, if possible. Bloom dates range from mid- to late-September.

Spider chrysanthemums: Tightly rolled petals give this type a unique appearance. Many varieties are not hardy and must be greenhouse-grown. There are a few, however—including Geisha Girl (lilac), which blooms late-September on 24-inch stems, and Sun Spider in mid-September—that are reliably hardy as far north as zone 5 if given winter protection.

Spoon chrysanthemums: So-called by reason of their petals—tight tubes which open out at tips to a spoon shape. Heights vary from 18 to 24 inches. Give winter protection in colder climates.

For photos of some chrysanthemum varieties and illustrated instructions on how to plant and divide mums, see pages 16 and 17.

CINQUEFOIL
see potentilla

COLUMBINE
(Aquilegia sp.)

ZONE: 3 **HEIGHT:** 24 to 30 inches
FLOWER COLOR: yellow, red, pink, blue, white
BLOOM TIME: June
LIGHT: sun, part-sun
PROPAGATION: seed or root starts

The native American wildflower *Aquilegia canadensis* and its hybridized relatives form an admirable group of hardy perennials that deserve a place in the mixed border. The native plant has red sepals and yellow spurs on flowers that dance to the slightest breeze on 12- to 24-inch stalks. It needs full sun and prefers rather dry, sandy soil, though it's tolerant of other kinds.

Its hybrid relatives include varieties with yellow, white, blue, rose, and crimson bloom. McKana Hybrids, a recent strain, comes in

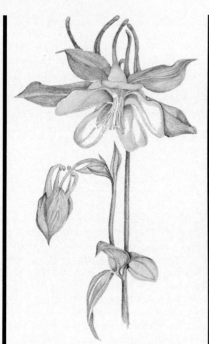

bright colors and grows 30 inches tall. Hardy zone 4 southward. Seed comes in a mixture of colors.

A. caerulea, or Rocky Mountain columbine, is one of the loveliest of columbines, having long spurs and blooming on 1- to 2-foot stems.

Foliage of all columbines is fan-shaped in varying shades of green, depending on the variety.

To insure perennial quality, cut all spent bloom before it starts to make seed. When flowering period has ended, cut foliage back to about 4 inches. New growth will arise and the plant will be stronger.

Established plants are difficult to move or divide. To increase your supply, start new ones from seed sown in late summer, winter in a cold frame, and transplant to the garden when frost danger passes. Or, purchase new plants in spring.

CONEFLOWER
see rudbeckia

CORALBELLS
(Heuchera sanguinea); also called alum-root

ZONE: 3 **HEIGHT:** 18 inches
FLOWER COLOR: white, pink, red, chartreuse
BLOOM TIME: June-September
LIGHT: sun, part-sun
PROPAGATION: seed or root division

Attractive mounds of leaves make this an attractive plant in or out of bloom. But it blooms over such a long season that it's a valuable member of a mixed perennial border and equally good in separate beds. Leaf mound stays low (8 inches), but tall bloom spikes reach upward, loaded with tiny bell-shaped flowers. The coral or pinkish-red

color is most common, and the one from which the plant takes its species name—sanguinea. But there are other attractive kinds such as White Cloud with creamy-white bells, and Chartreuse, with flowers of a soft chartreuse hue.

Heuchera plants perform best in a rich, moist, well-drained soil, but they grow satisfactorily in almost any kind of garden soil.

Smaller, new plants form around the base of the mother plant and make it easy for you to increase your supply. Dig up and divide about every three years, separating new plants from old. Replant 12 inches apart.

COREOPSIS
(Coreopsis sp.); also known as perennial tickseed

ZONE: 4 **HEIGHT:** 16 to 30 inches
FLOWER COLOR: yellow
BLOOM TIME: August to frost
LIGHT: full sun
PROPAGATION: seed or root division

With daisy-like flowers on plants that are mostly in the 20- to 30-inch range, coreopsis make choice additions to the mixed perennial border because they stay in bloom for such a long period of time. And they're not fussy about soil type.

There are both single and double varieties to choose from. Baby Sun, a dwarf, covers 16- to 18-inch plants with golden bloom all summer.

To grow from seed, plant in late summer in a cold frame or in a protected place. Transplant into the perennial border after all frost danger has passed. You may grow seed indoors in early spring, transplanting to the garden when frost danger has passed, with a good chance of getting some bloom during the first season.

Or, you can send for roots in spring from a mail-order nursery.

CORNFLOWER
see centaurea

CRANESBILL GERANIUM
see geranium

CUPID'S-DART
(Catananche caerulea)

ZONE: 4 **HEIGHT:** 15 to 18 inches
FLOWER COLOR: blue, white
BLOOM TIME: July-September
LIGHT: sun, part-sun
PROPAGATION: seed or root division

The common name of this hardy garden perennial comes from the Greek use of the plant in making love potions. Today the plant is grown for its bloom, which makes good bouquet material and is easily dried for winter arrangements.

Flowers are reminiscent of blue cornflowers borne on stems that rise above rosettes of green leaves.

Sow seeds indoors in early spring and transplant seedlings in the garden after the weather is frost-free. Or, sow directly in the garden after the soil warms. If you have an established clump of cupid's-dart, you can divide plants in the spring.

D

DAYLILIES
(Hemerocallis sp.)

ZONE: 2 **HEIGHT:** 20 to 48 inches
FLOWER COLOR: yellow, orange, pink, red
BLOOM TIME: summer-autumn
LIGHT: sun, part-sun, part-shade
PROPAGATION: root division

"Beautiful for a day" is the translation of the Greek word for this beautiful and trouble-free plant, but it's a misleading way to describe the bloom habits of the daylily. Since each flower stalk is loaded with buds, as one opens, blooms for a day, then dies, others are growing larger, ready to open on succeeding days.

Daylilies have received intensive hybridizing for a good many years, and collectors who pride themselves on having each new introduction in their garden will need ample bankrolls. When a new variety is first offered, it's obviously in short supply and may command up to $75 or more for a division.

But for the average gardener, there are so many old favorites on the market that cost need never be important. Actually, if the plant has been on the market a number of years, it has proven itself, though its price has grown small. As little as $1.50 can buy you a strong division of a sturdy favorite that will rapidly increase in your own garden in a few years' time.

In selecting daylilies, consider color, height, and season of bloom. This last-named feature is important if you want a long blooming season. The early daylilies will start to bloom in June; mid-season varieties, in July-August; and late daylilies that begin blooming in August carry on well into September, though this group is much smaller than the mid-season.

Plant catalogs will indicate whether the bloom stays "open evenings"—important if you'd like some to decorate the table. Look, too, for indications of "repeat bloom." Some that bloom early put on a second late show.

Although daylilies are undemanding as to soil type, it's wise to fertilize them in fall or very early spring. Set each new plant a foot away from its neighbor. Plants can be moved at any time of the year without endangering their life, though the foliage may wilt a bit if you choose a hot summer day. The best time to lift and divide is early spring, when new shoots emerge.

For color illustrations of some varieties and additional cultural advice, see pages 12 and 13.

Both for appearance's sake and for the good of the plant (to prevent it from forming seed and wasting energy that otherwise would go to increasing plant size), it's good practice to pick off spent bloom regularly.

DELPHINIUM
(Delphinium sp.)

ZONE: 3 **HEIGHT:** to 8 feet
FLOWER COLOR: white, blue, yellow, pink, lavender
BLOOM TIME: June, repeat in autumn
LIGHT: sun
PROPAGATION: seed or root division

Spring is the time to plant delphiniums. It's best to start with sturdy nursery plants for the impressive hybrid varieties such as the famous Round Table series of Pacific Coast Hybrids, or the English Blackmore and Langdon Hybrids. If you choose to start from seed, sow indoors or in a cold frame in early spring.

When you order your plants or sow seeds, it's time to start preparing the outdoor bed that will receive them. Delphiniums are known as "heavy feeders," which means you must supply them with extremely rich soil. Cover the bed with at least 2 inches of well-rotted cow manure or compost, or a mixture of the two. Space this in to a depth of 6 to 8 inches. Next, spread 5-10-5 fertilizer in proportions recommended on package. Add an additional 2 inches of compost or manure, spade this in thoroughly, and soak the bed or wait for a heavy rain. When soil has dried enough to be workable, you're ready to set out new plants.

Space plants 2 feet apart, setting crown at soil level—not below. Water well after planting and, if natural rainfall does not do the job for you, continue watering on a regular basis until plant is well established. After bloom stalks form, keep soil around the roots well watered but avoid soaking the bloom unnecessarily.

Even when you set out all plants of the same hybrid strain, they'll bloom at different times—a virtue if you like to prolong the season.

Set stakes in place and be ready to fasten bloom stems to them well ahead of the time buds begin to open. Few sights are sadder than a fallen delphinium stem, in full bloom, all for lack of staking.

When bloom ends on each plant, cut bloom stalk off just below lowest bloom. New leaves will come up at the plant's base and, when this occurs, cut off remainder of stalk.

Many plants will produce a fall crop of bloom, though on much shorter stems than the first bloom.

To keep plants strong, it will be necessary to continue adding manure and compost to soil every year, in late fall or early spring.

DIANTHUS
(Dianthus sp.); also known as pinks

ZONE: 3-7   **HEIGHT:** 3 to 24 inches
FLOWER COLOR: pink, white, red
BLOOM TIME: summer
LIGHT: sun, part-sun
PROPAGATION: seed, cuttings, or division

The family of pinks is a large one, including both annual and perennial varieties. Carnations and sweet william are both members of the pink family, as are the gilly flowers which are mentioned by Shakespeare.

Some of the best are *Dianthus alpinus,* only 3 to 4 inches tall and a perfect candidate for rock gardens; and *D. allwoodi,* with very sweetly scented flowers, some double, in a mixture of colors. If you cut off spent bloom regularly, these plants will stay in nearly continuous bloom from June until September. This one is hardy from zone 3 southward. Stems reach 15 inches.

Sweet william, *D. barbatus,* hardy from zone 4 south, bears bloom in umbels of bright color at the top of 1½-foot stems. It's usually grown as a biennial, though it does seed itself in if growing conditions suit it and thus behaves as a perennial. When setting out new plants, space them 10 inches apart.

All pinks like sunny garden spots with good drainage and a soil that is neutral or tends slightly toward the alkaline side. If your soil is acidic, use lime to make it more alkaline.

Pinks are easy to grow from seed sown in the garden as soon as soil warms. You may also make cuttings of varieties or colors you especially like, rooting them in a non-organic material such as vermiculite and setting them into the garden when root growth is adequate. Another way to renew plants is to divide established clumps in the spring.

DICENTRA
see bleeding heart

DICTAMNUS
see gas plant

DORONICUM
(Doronicum cordatum); also known as leopard's-bane

ZONE: 4   **HEIGHT:** 24 inches
FLOWER COLOR: yellow
BLOOM TIME: spring
LIGHT: sun, part-shade
PROPAGATION: root division

Earliest to bloom of all the tribe of daisy-like plants, *Doronicum cordatum* is eye-catching when grown close to Virginia bluebells, *Mertensia virginica*. Like that plant, foliage of doronicum also tends to disappear during the summer, so locations should be marked.

The hardiest variety of the several doronicums available on the market is Madam Mason. It's undemanding as to soil type and will sometimes put on a second show of bloom if you cut off first bloom promptly as it fades. This variety usually holds its foliage all summer.

To ensure plant hardiness, clumps should be divided and reset at least every other year. Fertilize in late fall or very early spring.

DRAGONHEAD
see physostegia

DUSTY MILLER
see artemisia

E

ECHINOPS
see globe thistle

ENGLISH DAISY
see bellis

EUPATORIUM
see ageratum

EUPHORBIA
see spurge

F

FALSE DRAGONHEAD
see physostegia

FELICIA
(Felicia amelloides); also known as blue marguerite and blue daisy

ZONE: 5   **HEIGHT:** 1 to 3 feet
FLOWER COLOR: blue
BLOOM TIME: early summer to October
LIGHT: sun, part-shade
PROPAGATION: seed and cuttings

A tender perennial, felicia is best grown in climates where winters are mild, or else resown each spring as an annual. Its flowers resemble the common daisy and are as large as an inch across. The plant is a generous bloomer, supplying a source of cut flowers as well as color in the mixed perennial border.

When main bloom period ends in late summer, it is often possible to get a second, though sparser, flowering if you cut the entire plant back severely, inducing a burst of new growth.

Felicia can be grown from seed sown in early spring. It also self-sows if some bloom is not clipped off the plant, but let go to seed. Or, you can take cuttings of established plants.

FEVERFEW
(Chrysanthemum parthenium)

ZONE: 3   **HEIGHT:** to 30 inches
FLOWER COLOR: cream
BLOOM TIME: summer
LIGHT: sun, part-sun
PROPAGATION: root division

Some catalogs may list this perennial as matricaria. It's an old-fashioned flower, attractive when planted between brilliant clumps of flowering plants for contrast, and good also for bouquets, as it's long-lasting. Flower heads measure only about ¾ of an inch across, but many are borne on each stem. Foliage and bloom have a pleasantly aromatic scent.

If spent bloom is cut off promptly, feverfew usually blooms from June through September.

Clumps increase in size and ought to be lifted, divided, and replanted about every third year.

FILIPENDULA
see meadowsweet

FLAX
(Linum sp.)

ZONE: 4 **HEIGHT:** 12 to 18 inches
FLOWER COLOR: blue, yellow
BLOOM TIME: summer
LIGHT: full sun
PROPAGATION: seed, cuttings, or root division

Although most cultivated types of flax are of medium height, there is a dwarf form, *Linum perenne alpinum*, suited to the rock garden and bearing blue flowers in spring.

Other more commonly grown and longer blooming kinds include *L. flavum* which blooms profusely all summer, with feathery foliage and showy yellow flowers on 15-inch stems. A cultivated variety, Heavenly Blue, produces brightest blue flowers on 12- to 18-inch stems and has recurring periods of bloom all summer, especially if spent flowers are promptly cut and plants are not allowed to go to seed.

Blue flax makes a lovely companion to white phlox, white campanula, and cream-colored feverfew.

Increase your supply of plants by dividing in early spring. Set divisions 8 to 10 inches apart. Or, take cuttings and root them. Plants started from seeds sown in spring seldom bloom until the second year.

FLEABANE
(Erigeron sp.)

ZONE: 3 **HEIGHT:** 10 to 36 inches
FLOWER COLOR: pink, lavender, white, blue, orange
BLOOM TIME: summer
LIGHT: sun, part-shade
PROPAGATION: root division

The fleabanes are undemanding as far as soil is concerned, and adapt easily to varying light conditions.

Members of the family that are good subjects for mixed flower borders include *Erigeron coulteri* or mountain daisy, hardy zone 6 southward and bearing white or

lavender bloom in summer; *E. aurantiacus*, which produces orange blooms and grows just 10 inches high; and *E. speciosus*, showy or Oregon fleabane (zone 4), with rose, lilac, or white blooms resembling those of hardy asters. This species and its cultivars will bloom mid- to late-summer. Hybridized varieties to consider include Azure Fairy. Its lavender flowers are semi-double and are borne on 30-inch stems. It is in constant bloom for most of June and July. Forrester's Darling has bright pink semi-double flowers with the same growth habits as *E. speciosus* (zone 3).

G

GAILLARDIA
(Gaillardia aristata); also known as blanket flower

ZONE: 3 **HEIGHT:** 12 to 30 inches
FLOWER COLOR: gold, orange, red
BLOOM TIME: summer
LIGHT: full sun
PROPAGATION: root division

Good border plants, most varieties fit into mid-border locations. Gaillardia also is rewarding as a cut flower.

A rich though light and well-drained soil gets the best results from this showy plant. But it will tolerate quite sandy soil and seaside conditions. There is also an annual gaillardia.

Hybrid perennials that make fine border plants include Burgundy, with wine-red bloom that can be as large as 3 inches across and reach 30 inches in height; Monarch strain, which comes in a range of colors; and Yellow Queen, its name accurately describing its color.

Goblin, a dwarf variety, is only 8 to 12 inches tall, with dark red flowers bordered in yellow. It blooms from July onward.

Should your plant fail to send up new foliage the spring after planting, do not discard the root. Dig it up, and divide and replant the divisions from 10 to 12 inches apart. The crown of the plant may be dead; if so, discard that section only.

GAS PLANT
(Dictamnus sp.)

ZONE: 3 **HEIGHT:** 1½ to 2½ feet
FLOWER COLOR: white, pink
BLOOM TIME: summer
LIGHT: sun
PROPAGATION: buy started plants or sow from seed

The odd name of this favorite garden perennial comes from the fact that, on a hot night when no breezes are stirring, you can often produce a small burst of flame if you hold a lighted match over the blooms.

Once established, dictamnus is very long lived, but don't try to move an established plant; you will probably lose the plant if you do.

Since dictamnus is not easy to raise from seed, you will probably have the best luck if you start with a purchased young plant. Plants grow slowly, but do eventually grow into big clumps, so allow for this by spacing 3 feet apart in locations where you want permanent growth. If you do start from seed, sow in the spring or fall and let seedlings grow for a full garden season before attempting to move them.

Provide a sunny and well-drained location for dictamnus. They bloom during June and July, but the foliage remains attractive after the flowering season has passed. Late blooming bearded iris and spuria iris are enhanced by being planted close to clumps of dictamnus.

Dictamnus albus grows about 30 inches tall with spikes of white flowers in June and July. *D. albus rubra* puts up pink bloom but resembles the white variety in every other way. Both are about 30 inches tall at maturity and are also good to use as cut flowers.

GAYFEATHER

see liatris

GENTIAN
(Gentiana sp.)

ZONE: 4 **HEIGHT:** 4 to 18 inches
FLOWER COLOR: blue, violet, rarely white or yellow
BLOOM TIME: July-September
LIGHT: light shade
PROPAGATION: cuttings or root division

The original gentians were mountain flowers brought to

English gardens long ago, then hybridized to a considerable extent to produce a few varieties that grow as tall as 18 inches. The mountain species were mostly dwarf, and descendants are still in use, largely as rock garden specimens.

Considered rather difficult to establish, gentians have been known to take as long as a year to germinate. It is, therefore, much better to purchase young plants than to try to grow them from seed.

It is probably unwise to attempt to grow this beautiful plant if you live in areas with long, hot, and dry summers.

Gentiana lutea is the yellow variety of the gentian group, rarely offered in plant catalogs. *G. andrewsi,* also called the closed or bottle gentian, is one of the most widely grown members of the family. Flowers are a deep purplish-blue. They bloom in July and August if planted in moist soil, and will tolerate light shade. *G. saponaria* is also fairly widely cultivated. It has blue flowers borne on solitary stems 8 to 18 inches in height in autumn.

The fringed gentian, a wildflower celebrated in verse, is an endangered species. Under no circumstances should it be picked or dug if encountered in the wild. It's offered by a few plantsmen who deal in wildflowers.

GERANIUM

(Geranium sp.); also known as cranesbill geranium

ZONE: 4 **HEIGHT:** dwarf to 10 in.
FLOWER COLOR: pink, red, purple
BLOOM TIME: early spring
LIGHT: sun
PROPAGATION: root division

Several members of this true geranium family (what we most often refer to as geraniums are really pelargoniums) make ideal rockery plants or edgings at the front of a mixed border. So long as there is good drainage, they will grow in any soil.

Of the dwarf forms, *Geranium cinereum 'splendens'* has deep pink blooms, but grows only 3 inches tall and is not hardy north of zone 6. *G. dalmaticum* has pale pink bloom veined with crimson. It spreads rapidly, but is not difficult to keep in control by pulling unwanted young plants as they appear at the edges of the main plant. In fall, leaves turn red, making spots of welcome color when most perennials are no longer in bloom.

G. himalayense produces purplish flowers on 10-inch stems, and continues to bloom from May to August. *G. sanguineum,* a European native, is generous with its red-purple flowers, also from May to August. Cut tops back after the first heavy bloom period and roots will send up new shoots. If you want more of this plant, simply allow it to go to seed.

Propagate any of these geraniums by division in either late fall or in early spring.

GERBERA

(Gerbera jamesoni); also known as transvaal daisy

ZONE: 8 **HEIGHT:** 18 inches
FLOWER COLOR: cream, pink, yellow, rose, orange-red, violet
BLOOM TIME: summer
LIGHT: sun, part-shade
PROPAGATION: seed, root division, or cuttings

Not for harsh climates, these showy plants can be grown well in zones 8 through 10. Bloom may be as large as 4 inches across, on stems tall enough to make them valuable as cut flowers.

Gray-green foliage grows in the form of a basal rosette from which flower stems emerge.

Purchase roots unless you're ready to wait a year for bloom from seed. Or, you can root cuttings taken from side shoots. Set roots so crown is at soil level or just above, and plant in late fall.

Clumps should be lifted, divided, and replanted every three to four years. Plant 8 to 10 inches apart.

In the north, gerbera makes a good, cool greenhouse plant, supplying bloom in spring from roots planted in pots late in the preceding summer.

GEUM

(Geum sp.); also known as avens

ZONE: 5 **HEIGHT:** 1 ½ to 2 feet
FLOWER COLOR: yellow, orange, scarlet
BLOOM TIME: summer
LIGHT: full sun
PROPAGATION: seed or root division

Not for hot climates, this plant requires a rich, well-drained soil full of organic matter such as leaf mold or compost that will retain moisture during summer months. Clumps increase in size, but rather slowly; the plants should reach maturity within three years.

Hardy to zone 5 if provided with winter protection is Heldreichi geum, with bold foliage up to 12 inches and double orange flowers on 18-inch stems.

Lady Stratheden, developed from a Chilean cultivar, has yellow, double bloom on 2-foot stems, and is not hardy north of zone 6.

Mrs. Bradshaw (zone 6) has bright red flowers on 2-foot stems.

These plants put on their main show of bloom in June and July, but some bloom may occur up to October.

They can be grown from seed sown in late summer, wintered over in a cold frame, and set into the garden after all danger of frost has passed.

GLOBEFLOWER
(Trollius europaeus)

ZONE: 3   **HEIGHT:** 30 inches
FLOWER COLOR: yellow, orange
BLOOM TIME: May-June
LIGHT: part-shade
PROPAGATION: seed or root division

Large flowers of ball shape on tall, sturdy stems make this a most desirable plant if you can supply the moist, partly shady location it needs.

Spade in plenty of humus before planting, and mulch to retain moisture during hot months.

Byrnes Giant has deep yellow flowers of large size, and Prichard's Giant is similar, but a deeper shade of golden-yellow. Golden Nugget *(Trollius ledebouri)* blooms from June to August.

Foliage is attractive even when the plant is not in bloom, and cut flowers are long-lasting. Plants often send up sporadic bloom well after the major season is past.

Set plants 8 to 10 inches apart and let them serve as complements to late-blooming iris and June-blooming lily varieties. They are most attractive when set out in groups of three or more. Plant in spring when soil has warmed. Trollius are not difficult to grow from seed sown outdoors in spring, but will provide no bloom until the following year.

GLOBE THISTLE
(Echinops exaltatus)

ZONE: 4   **HEIGHT:** 4 feet
FLOWER COLOR: blue; (foliage is silvery)
BLOOM TIME: July
LIGHT: sun, part-sun
PROPAGATION: seed or root division

Not to be confused with the farmer's pest, the Canadian thistle, the globe thistle is a highly

recommended hardy perennial for back-of-the-border placement.

Any ordinary garden soil will be suitable, and they grow well in either full sun or light shade. The flower heads are globe-shaped.

Use globe thistles of the variety Taplow Blue as the perfect accompaniment to yellow daylilies that bloom at the same time. Bloom is also one to dry for fall arrangements. Cut stems to desired length and hang, head down, in a cool, dry place out of sunlight so the blue color won't fade.

Set young plants into the border in spring, when ground has warmed.

GOLDENROD
see solidago

GYPSOPHILA
see baby's-breath

H

HELENIUM
(Helenium autumnale); also known as false sunflower or sneeze-weed

ZONE: 3   **HEIGHT:** 3 to 4 feet
FLOWER COLOR: yellow, mixed gold, red
BLOOM TIME: late-summer
LIGHT: sun
PROPAGATION: seed, root division, or cuttings

A valuable member of any mixed border of perennial plants, helenium gives its major burst of color at a time when little else is in bloom—August into September. It's tolerant of soil—almost any type will do—and takes heat well.

The brilliant variety starts to bloom about the middle of August and goes on for the next six weeks. The flowers are a mixture of reds and oranges—the colors of turning leaves. Bruno sports deep mahogany-red flowers. Butterpat is solid-colored—a rich, clear yellow.

Heleniums are good plants to supply cut flowers when most phlox are gone and chrysanthemums haven't yet begun their show. They grow vigorously and benefit from being lifted, divided, and replanted in early spring every other year.

HELIANTHUS

(Helianthus decapetalus multiflorus); also known as perennial sunflower

ZONE: 4   **HEIGHT:** 3 feet
FLOWER COLOR: pale to deep yellow
BLOOM TIME: July to frost
LIGHT: sun
PROPAGATION: seed or root division

Well suited to any sunny, dry spot in your garden, the helianthus bloom resembles small sunflowers (it's a relative of the annual sunflower). Although it survives

drought, it produces lots more bloom when watered regularly.

The multiflorus variety sold by nurseries will give you big sprays of nearly double flowers from July on.

This plant probably is best grown in a bed to itself because it grows rampantly and could become a pest in a mixed border.

Set out plants in spring. Or sow seed in spring, but don't expect bloom until the next year.

HELIOPSIS

(Heliopsis helianthoides); also known as oxeye

ZONE: 3   **HEIGHT:** to 5 feet
FLOWER COLOR: yellow, orange
BLOOM TIME: summer
LIGHT: sun, part-sun
PROPAGATION: division or cuttings

Another of the late-summer flowering perennials, heliopsis is entirely hardy and is especially welcome because it fills a garden gap, flowering after most perennials have finished the season, but before chrysanthemums come into bloom.

Its culture is the same as that of helianthus, but it is less-often grown

because of the availability of a wider selection of good plants among the genus helianthus. One variety of heliopsis, however, does deserve more attention than it receives: pitcheriana. This is a dwarf, bushier than the taller varieties and reaching only 2 to 3 feet in height. It is well-suited to the perennial border and also valuable as a source of cut flowers. It tolerates drought and does well even in dry places.

Similar to pitcheriana is scabra, sporting deep yellow flowers with dark centers. Blooms measure up to 3 inches across, appear from July until frost, and are good both as cut flowers and in dried arrangements. The mature plant is 3 feet tall.

To keep your plants in peak shape, divide every three years. If you want more plants but don't want to divide clumps, take cuttings during the summer.

HEMEROCALLIS

see daylily

HELLEBORUS

also known as Christmas rose *(Helleborus niger)* or Lenten rose *(H. orientalis)*

ZONE: 4   **HEIGHT:** 12 inches
FLOWER COLOR: white, pink, purple, green
BLOOM TIME: late fall to spring
LIGHT: shade
PROPAGATION: sow seeds in early fall, or divide

Ideally, helleborus should be grown in the shade of trees, since it requires moist, woodsy soil that's rich in humus. Add leaf mold and well-rotted cow manure if your soil is not up to the needs of this plant.

The season of bloom depends very much on the weather. Long, mild falls with ample rainfall might permit bloom of Christmas rose in late autumn.

Where killing frost comes early, the plant must be protected. A discarded storm window turned into a cold frame-like structure, with bricks to support it, works well. Mulch with marsh hay or straw.

In such cases, bloom will probably not come until spring. It should also be kept in mind that the plant matures quite slowly and will not be able to produce bloom until the second or third season. Once this plant is established, do not move unless it's essential. If you must move plants, or want to divide them, wait until August or September. Lift plants carefully, taking care not to break the brittle roots.

HOSTA
(Hosta sp.); also known as plantain lily or funkia

ZONE: 3   **HEIGHT:** dwarf to 30 in.
FLOWER COLOR: white, blue, violet, lilac
BLOOM TIME: July-August
LIGHT: shade, part-shade
PROPAGATION: divison or seed

As an extremely decorative and easy-to-grow plant for shaded areas, it's difficult to think of any that can rival the hostas. Grown primarily for their foliage, the many species and varieties bloom at various times from early to late summer.

Some have sweet-scented bloom in the form of pendant bell-shaped flowers on tall stems that emerge from the rosette mat of foliage. Probably the most outstanding hosta for fragrant bloom is *Hosta plantaginea 'grandiflora'*, which shows very fragrant flowers on 30-inch stems in late August and September. This one is somewhat less hardy than the rest and should be planted in spring rather than fall. Give it winter protection the first year. Thereafter, it will satisfactorily adapt to colder weather.

Other hostas to grow for their handsome foliage include: *H. decorata 'marginata'*, oval green leaves enhanced by a white margin, with lavender bloom in August on 20-inch stems; *H. fortunei 'viridis-marginata'*, oval leaves of chartreuse hue in spring, gradually becoming a solid light green in summer; *H. lancifolia* with much narrower leaves than most hostas—a shiny dark green in color and producing lavender flowers on 2-foot stems in late August or early September; *H. sieboldi,* also known as the seersucker hosta, which grows 2 to 3 feet high and has huge leaves marked with overall puckered patterns; and *H. undulata,* with wavy green and white variegated foliage.

Although hostas like rich, moist soil, they survive hot dry spells and perform adequately in quite poor garden soils.

Clumps of hosta increase in size each year and are easy to divide. In a few years' time, you can easily double your supply of any particular variety. This is a real virtue if you become a hosta addict and begin

to buy some of the new, high-priced introductions. Trading more expensive plants with other hosta fanciers makes the hobby less expensive to pursue.

Varieties listed here, however, have been long on the market and are not in the "high priced" group. Use them as a ground cover under shade trees, as edgings for shaded driveways, and in separate beds of several varieties so planted as to make pleasing contrasts of size, leaf shape, and hue.

HYPERICUM
(Hypericum patulum); also known as St. John's wort

ZONE: 5   **HEIGHT:** 2 to 3 feet
FLOWER COLOR: yellow
BLOOM TIME: May-August
LIGHT: sun, part-sun
PROPAGATION: division or cuttings

The large genus of hypericum includes a great many varieties of shrubs and sub-shrubs (woody stems), but only a few are of interest as garden perennials. All of them tolerate a sandy soil.

One variety well suited to use in the mixed perennial border is Hidcote, which freely produces its yellow flowers that may be as large as 2 inches across. Foliage tends to be evergreen, though even if it dies back, new growth will come up from the roots in spring and produce bloom by midsummer. Given good winter protection, it has been known to survive in zone 4, though there it must be winter-protected, and will probably die back anyway. Other reliable varieties are Sun Goddess and Sungold—both reaching heights of 3 to 4 feet.

Divide early in the spring, or take cuttings anytime.

I

IBERIS

see candytuft

ICELAND POPPY

(Papaver nudicaule)

ZONE: 2-5   **HEIGHT:** 12 inches
FLOWER COLOR: white, pink, red, yellow, orange
BLOOM TIME: May
LIGHT: sun, part-sun
PROPAGATION: seed

This poppy, as its common name indicates, had its origin in the arctic areas and is most rewarding in areas

where summers are fairly cool. It also may be grown as a winter annual in the South.

If you live where summers are apt to be long, hot, and dry, forget the Iceland poppy and turn to its relative, the Oriental poppy, for gorgeous early-summer bloom.

Dainty flowers 3 inches across and sweetly fragrant are in bloom at the same time as many of the hardy bulbs, and are pretty in the spring mixed-perennial garden.

In the North, sow seed in early spring and expect some flowers the first season, with full bloom from the plants the second year.

Further south, sow seed in early autumn for early spring bloom. In warm areas, treat the plant as an annual.

INDIGO

see Baptisia

IRIS

(Iris sp.)

ZONE: 3 south   **HEIGHT:** dwarf to 38 inches
FLOWER COLOR: white, yellow, orange, red, pink, rose, lavender, purple, blue
BLOOM TIME: spring and summer
LIGHT: sun, part-sun
PROPAGATION: division

The iris tribe is so vast that it is extremely difficult to generalize about, except to say that its members are among the most beautiful perennials you can possibly find for your garden and that there are some kinds that will grow well for you almost anywhere.

There are bulbous, tuberous, and rhizotomatous kinds. But for the purpose of this discussion, iris will be presented by the following classes: bulbous, tall bearded, dwarf bearded, Dutch, Japanese, Siberian, and spuria, with recommended varieties listed and described.

For color photographs and further cultural information on iris, see pages 8 and 9.

The Bulbous Iris

Beardless dwarfs remain reasonably perennial in zone 4 with winter protection, but more

dependably so in zones 5 to 8. Plant beardless iris in the fall. *Iris danfordiae,* with vivid yellow flowers not much bigger than a hybrid crocus, may appear as early as late February, according to the season, but certainly by early March. This, of course, makes them subject to possible frost damage in colder zones, though it does not normally kill the bulb.

Both danfordiae and reticulata iris grow only 4 to 6 inches tall. Use them at the front of a mixed border or in a rock garden. Let foliage ripen naturally.

I. reticulata Joyce has large flowers for its class, with pale blue falls blotched with orange and blue uprights; Violet Beauty is deep purple with an orange blotch, and Spring Time is pale blue with white markings on the dark blue falls. Reticulata iris want an alkaline soil; if yours is on the acidic side, dust with lime after the blooming period ends each year.

Both danfordiae and reticulata iris grow only 4 to 6 inches tall. Use them at the front of a mixed border or in a rock garden. Let foliage ripen and turn yellow naturally.

47

Dutch iris, also bulbous, may be grown successfully in the garden in zones 5 and 6, but success is doubtful if temperatures sink below zero. If you decide to try your luck with Dutch iris, purchase only a few bulbs to begin with and see how you fare. Plant 3 inches deep and 4 inches apart. The variety *I. xiphium* Franz Hals sports violet standards and violet-bronze falls; Sunshine is solidly bright yellow; pale blue Wedgwood has yellow blotches on the falls; and White Perfection makes a good neighbor to any of the colored varieties.

Tall Bearded Iris

This iris group abounds in such a multitude of spectacular beauties that it's hard to choose among them, except on the basis of colors you want. Almost all in this category are reliably hardy in zones 3 and 4 if winter protection is provided. Plant all bearded iris in the fall.

These iris must have good drainage or rhizomes will rot. Depth of planting is very important: rhizome should be barely below soil surface. If planted too deep, there will be no bloom. It's best practice to prepare the bed for iris some weeks before planting. Spade a fertilizer with a low nitrogen count into the soil at about an ounce to the square foot. Also dig in compost or well-rotted manure, though this shouldn't touch the rhizomes as it may cause infection. Topdress each plant in spring with superphosphate—about ¼ cup to each plant.

Bearded iris should be lifted, divided, and replanted about every five years. Follow directions on fertilizing the soil as for initial planting, keep weeds away from the base of plants, and retain soil moisture with mulch.

The one serious cultural problem tall bearded iris present is the likelihood that they'll be infested by iris borers. If you are loath to resort to insecticides, you can get rid of this pest by lifting any plant whose leaves display a telltale wet-looking streak, and searching for, cutting out, and destroying the borer before replanting the rhizome. The only other method of control is to use a contact insecticide each spring when new growth is about 3 inches tall, repeating twice more at weekly intervals. This method will not kill any borers already present, but will prevent new infection.

Dwarf Bearded Varieties

Mostly 10 to 12 inches tall, the dwarf iris tend to flower early—in May in all but the most northerly zones. Many are sweet-scented. Use them in the rock garden or at the front of mixed perennial borders.

Gleaming Gold is 12 inches tall and a very brilliant yellow; Bright White matches its name to perfection, and is only 10 inches tall; Pepita, also ten-inch, is a lovely gentian blue with a deeper blotch on the falls.

Dwarf bearded iris may be planted in either spring or fall.

Japanese Iris

I. kaempferi belong in general to the beardless group, but are a quite distinct category within that group. The Japanese have developed the Higo strain that has startlingly large bloom—as wide as 8 inches across—growing on stems tall enough to qualify as important back-of-the-border plants. Some varieties are as tall as 4 to 5 feet. Most bloom in June.

Japanese iris prefer moist soil but cannot tolerate standing water. Nor can they take acidic soil. Use lime to neutralize yours if it's naturally on the acidic side.

Plants multiply fairly quickly, so you can increase your supply by lifting, dividing, and replanting about every three years.

Among the Higo strain, these are a few of the outstanding varieties: Ise, with a 6- to 8-inch bloom of very pale blue, veined with purple and yellow at the base of petals; Nara, with 8- to 9-inch double flowers of deep violet color that bloom in July, a little later than most, on sturdy, 40-inch stems; and Over the Waves, with very ruffled petals of pure white edged in pale purple, borne on 4- to 5-foot stems.

Siberian Iris

Easiest to grow of all iris and seldom attacked by any pests are the Siberian iris, (*I. siberica*). Prepare the bed for these plants by digging down about 12 inches and enriching soil with humus, compost, or peat moss along with a fertilizer low in nitrogen.

In established clumps, roots go deep, making plants drought-resistant. Clumps continue to grow in size, but do not require digging and separating to remain vigorous. Of course, you may separate plants if you want to repeat identical clumps throughout the length of a mixed border—something that is quite effective.

Older varieties such as Perry's Blue, Caesar's Brother (purple), and Snow Queen are still very much worth growing. Plants remain in bloom for two to three weeks in June, and supply bouquets to take indoors. All grow to about 3 feet in height with dark green foliage that remains attractive when bloom ends. All prefer sun but will bloom in part-shade.

In making original plantings of Siberian iris, plant several single divisions from 3 to 4 inches apart to form a clump.

Among the newer introductions in the Siberian iris group—most of which are slightly taller than the older kinds already mentioned—Blue Brilliant is an especially attractive variety, growing to 39 inches. *I. s.* Cambridge has big turquoise-color bloom on stems 36 inches tall. And *I. s.* Lights of Paris, with yellow centers, reaches a height of 35 inches.

Spuria Iris

Hardiest of any of the herbaceous irises, the spurias are also the last of the iris tribe to bloom, following on the heels of the late tall bearded kinds. They belong to the beardless group and grow as tall as 36 to 50 inches, with sturdy green spear-like leaves that remain attractive long after the bloom is gone.

Spurias need good drainage, soil that's rich in compost, and deeper planting than do the bearded kinds.

Cover strong roots with 2 inches of soil and place them in full sun, if possible. You will not need to dig up and divide this iris—just let clumps increase naturally. Plant in fall for the root development that must take place before you can get bloom. Don't expect spectacular amounts of bloom for the first year or two; but from then on you'll be able to cut big, long-lasting bouquets.

Recommended varieties include solid yellow Sunny Days, pale blue Morning Tide, and ruffled white Wake Robin.

J

JACOB'S-LADDER
(Polemonium caeruleum); also known as Greek valerian

ZONE: 4 **HEIGHT:** 1½ feet
FLOWER COLOR: blue
BLOOM TIME: spring
LIGHT: shade, part-shade
PROPAGATION: self-sown seed, division

Clusters of sky-blue flowers and attractive ferny foliage make Jacob's ladder an excellent companion to narcissus, as they bloom at about the same time. Totally undemanding about soil type, they need some shade and moisture. There is a white variety of this plant, *Polemonium caeruleum album,* though it is less attractive in most garden placements than the blue one.

There is also the relative *P. reptans,* sometimes called by the common name of bluebell, which grows 2 feet tall and also bears clusters of drooping blue flowers. The culture is the same as for *P. caeruleum,* and it blooms at approximately the same time.

Polemoniums self-sow readily. Pull out unwanted plants or transplant to a new location where you want to establish a stand.

JUPITER'S-BEARD
(Centranthus ruber); also known as red valerian

ZONE: 4 **HEIGHT:** 3 feet
FLOWER COLOR: rose, white
BLOOM TIME: summer
LIGHT: sun, part-sun
PROPAGATION: seed or root division

No plant could bloom more reliably than the red valerian; it produces clusters of flowers in midsummer with little effort on your part.

On all counts, Ruber variety is a very satisfactory perennial that grows 3 feet tall and bears its sweet-scented rose flowers on 30-inch stems.

You can increase your supply of this plant by lifting, dividing, and transplanting divisions in early spring. But the plant is also a generous self-sower, so you may need do nothing but wait for it to increase by its own seed. If you don't want plants to spread, pull seedlings.

Albus is the white form of this same plant, and has the same form and habits, except that it does not produce much seed.

Set out new plants in spring, spacing 18 inches apart. Average garden soil is satisfactory.

K

KNIPHOFIA
see poker plant

L

LAMB'S-EARS
see stachys

LAVENDER
(Lavandula angustifolia)

ZONE: 5 **HEIGHT:** 15 to 30 inches
FLOWER COLOR: blue, lavender
BLOOM TIME: mid- to late-summer
LIGHT: sun
PROPAGATION: seed, divisions, stem cuttings

Lavender is one of the most fragrant plants in border or herb gardens. There are three commonly grown varieties. English or true lavender, the showiest, produces the most fragrant flowers and is often used in potpourris and sachets. Spike lavender produces larger, more fragrant leaves. And French lavender, slightly less popular, is grown primarily as a bath fragrance.

Start seeds of all varieties indoors ten to twelve weeks before the last expected frost. Germination and survival rates are low, so be sure to sow extra seeds, or plant stem cuttings or divisions from established plants. Plant seedlings outdoors in a sunny location after all danger of frost is passed.

Harvest fresh leaves as needed and flower heads before they open. Hang cut stems upside down in a shady, well ventilated area until dry. In cold climate areas, mulch with 2 to 3 inches of leaves or straw for winter protection.

LEADWORT
(Ceratostigma plumbaginoides); also known as plumbago

ZONE: 6 **HEIGHT:** 1 foot
FLOWER COLOR: blue
BLOOM TIME: August-September
LIGHT: sun, part-shade
PROPAGATION: division or cuttings

Bright blue phlox-like bloom and shiny green leaves recommend this plant as a ground cover or as an edging at the front of mixed borders. Leadwort is also effective in rock gardens.

Foliage turns an attractive bronze color in fall. Plants require well-drained soil, and need winter protection if grown as far north as zone 6.

Set plants 1 to 2 feet apart; they'll spread fairly rapidly by means of underground roots, and are easy to propagate by division.

LENTEN ROSE
see helleborus

LIATRIS
(Liatris sp.); also known as gayfeather

ZONE: 3 **HEIGHT:** 4 feet
FLOWER COLOR: rose, purple, white
BLOOM TIME: summer-autumn
LIGHT: sun, light shade
PROPAGATION: seed or root division

Not widely used, this native of North America deserves more attention for use in the mixed perennial border. It's also good for cutting and drying.

Liatris pycnostachya has purple flowers on 4-foot stems in July and August. *L. scariosa* White Spire has white flowers on 40-inch stems, blooming in August and continuing well into September. *L. spicata montana* Kobold is a dwarf and grows only from 18 to 24 inches tall. Its red-purple bloom begins in July and continues to September.

An undemanding and hardy perennial, gayfeather likes light soils that are on the sandy side.

LILIES, HARDY
(Lilium sp.)

ZONE: 3 **HEIGHT:** 2 to 8 feet
FLOWER COLOR: white, orange, red, salmon, yellow, maroon, pink, crimson
BLOOM TIME: June-September, depending on variety
LIGHT: sun to part-sun
PROPAGATION: bulbs

All lilies demand well-drained soil and like to have their "heads in the sun, feet in the shade." This makes hardy lilies perfect candidates for mixed perennial borders, although they are just as handsome planted in groups by themselves, with hedges as background. Plant lilies in the fall.

Except for the martagons and the Madonna lilies, lily bulbs should be planted from 4 to 8 inches deep, measuring from the base of the lily bulb. The Madonna lily should be covered with not more than an inch of soil and should put up top growth before frost if they are to bloom the following season. Plant martagon lilies about 2 inches deep.

It's important to remember that lilies are never truly dormant, and so should be planted promptly when you buy or receive a shipment.

When planting, add a handful of bone meal to the bottom of each hole you dig. After covering the bulb with soil, spread the planting bed with a 2- to 3-inch layer of straw for winter protection and early weed control in the spring.

50

If you use lilies in flower arrangements, don't cut longer stems than you need. Severe cutting can cause loss of the plant. Lilies need stems and leaves to build up bulb strength for next season's bloom.

It's not harmful to cut off individual lilies to float in decorative bowls and dishes. Also, cut off spent flowers, leaving stems and leaves intact.

A good lily collection should include early, mid-season and late-blooming varieties for a continuous display of color. Some of the most popular, disease-resistant varieties of hardy lilies include:

Early flowering—Bittersweet, Nova, Regal, Improved Strain, and Sonata.
Mid-season flowering—Imperial Crimson Strain, Pink Perfection Strain, Golden Splendor Strain, and Harlequin Hybrids.
Late-season flowering—Tiger Lily, Imperial Silver Strain, Imperial Gold Strain, and Redband Hybrids.

LINUM
see flax

LOBELIA
(Lobelia cardinalis); also called cardinal flower

ZONE: 2   **HEIGHT:** 24 to 30 in.
FLOWER COLOR: bright red
BLOOM TIME: late summer to early fall
LIGHT: shade
PROPAGATION: root division or stem cuttings in midsummer

Lobelia cardinalis is one of the handsomest of plants to grow in shade. Its tall, spike form makes it good for back-of-the-border.

It grows best planted in groups, and plants should be set 6 inches apart. Each plant will send up from four to six bloom spikes.

Another perennial lobelia also worth growing in shade is a variety called *L. spicata.* It has stems of about the same height as the cardinal flower, but its bloom is blue.

Less hardy than its relative, it is hardy in zone 4 with good winter protection. This one, too, is easily propagated by root division, either in early spring or in fall. It blooms from June to September.

LOOSESTRIFE
(Lythrum sp.)

ZONE: 3   **HEIGHT:** to 4 feet
FLOWER COLOR: pink, purple, red
BLOOM TIME: June to September
LIGHT: part-shade to full sun
PROPAGATION: root division in early spring, or cuttings

A long-time favorite in the tribe of lythrums is the vivid purple Dropmore, which blooms freely all summer long, with 20- to 36-inch spikes of bloom that recommend it for mid- or back-border placement.

Thick mulch pays dividends since the lythrums do best in moist soil, though they also require good drainage.

Morden's Gleam, as close to red as you will find among lythrums, grows as tall as 4 feet.

Morden's Pink flourishes in sunny locations. Each plant eventually grows into a clump as large as 3 feet wide, and 3 to 4 feet tall.

To insure the perennial nature of any lythrum variety, plants should be lifted, divided, and replanted every three years. Space plants 3 feet apart when making original plantings or when replanting divisions of old plants.

Although new plants may be set into the garden in either spring or fall, early spring is the time to divide older, established plants. After dividing, make sure newly set plants receive ample water the first year to encourage rapid growth of the new feeder root system.

LUNGWORT
(*Pulmonaria* sp.)

ZONE: 3   **HEIGHT:** 10 to 15 in.
FLOWER COLOR: blue, pink, rose
BLOOM TIME: April-May
LIGHT: shade or part-shade
PROPAGATION: division in early spring

Another common name of this valuable perennial is blue cowslip—more attractive than lungwort. But the latter name is more widely used, as folklore reveals that this plant was once believed efficacious in the treatment of diseases of the lungs.

There are several species in cultivation. Foliage of all plants in the lungwort family is splashed with silvery white blotches, and the plant is especially effective if planted near hardy spring bulbs in bloom during April and May.

Pulmonaria saccharata Pink Dawn does well in almost any soil, even if it is continuously moist. Flowers are an attractive shade of rosy pink.

Plants are from 12 to 15 inches tall and spread fairly rapidly. With frequent division, it's possible to start with a few plants and, in a few years' time, have enough to cover a large area. Set plants 10 inches apart.

The variety known as Mrs. Moon is very similar to Pink Dawn but is slightly shorter—from 10 to 12 inches tall. Its flowers start out pink, but gradually turn to blue as they open and mature.

Unlike Virginia bluebells which it resembles, the foliage of lungwort remains visible and attractive throughout the garden season (the foliage of Virginia bluebells ripens and disappears within a few weeks after blooming).

LUPINE
(*Lupinus* sp.)

ZONES: 4-7   **HEIGHT:** 3 to 5 feet
FLOWER COLOR: blue, pink, red, yellow, purple, also bi-colors in a wide variety of combinations
BLOOM TIME: spring into summer in temperate climates
LIGHT: full sun
PROPAGATION: seed or purchased plants

Wild varieties of lupine are found in temperate zones of many countries. But only the Russell Hybrids, developed by an English nurseryman, are well suited to growing in the mixed perennial

border, and then only if you live where summers are mild. These plants cannot take intense heat and hot winds.

Although it's possible to buy seed of the Russell Hybrids, the average gardener will prefer to buy plants, since it takes two years from planting before the plant flowers well.

Lupine bloom, borne on tall spikes, is sweetpea-like in form, and makes a striking impression planted in fairly large groups. When you purchase young plants that have been field-grown, you will probably not be offered an exact color choice, other than blue and white, and carmine or coppery shades. But as almost all of these colors are harmonious when planted next to each other, this will not be a great disadvantage to most gardeners.

If the climate is right—on the cool and moist side—the soil may be heavy or sandy and you will still get healthy growth with many long-lasting stalks of flowers.

LYCHNIS
(*Lychnis* sp.); also called catchfly
or Maltese-cross

ZONE: 3 **HEIGHT:** 12 to 36 in.
FLOWER COLOR: range of reds
BLOOM TIME: May through July
LIGHT: full sun
PROPAGATION: seed or division
   Related to the pinks, lychnis is a
valued summer perennial for the
mixed border. Big heads of brightly
colored bloom are attention-getters
at front- or mid-border locations,
depending upon the variety you
choose to grow.
   Foot-high *Lychnis Haageana*
hybrids put out blooms that can
measure as wide as 2 inches across.
Available in mixed colors only, these
include a range of salmons,
oranges, and reds that are all
compatible. Place at the front of the
border.

   The variety *L. chalcedoniia,*
known as scarlet Maltese-cross, is
from 2½ to 3 feet tall, with big
bloom heads on sturdy stalks, and is
effective at back-of-the-border
locations. Its main period of bloom
is in June and July. A very hardy
variety, it thrives in ordinary soil and
multiplies rapidly. Lift, divide, and
replant every three years, and allow
18 inches of space between newly
set plants.

   If you plan to grow lychnis from
seed, you may sow it in spring and
will probably have bloom by August
of the same season. Autumn-sown
seed will bloom the following spring,
in May or June.

LYTHRUM
see loosestrife

M-N

MEADOW RUE
see thalictrum

MEADOWSWEET
(*Filipendula vulgaris*); also called
dropwort

ZONE: 4 **HEIGHT:** 18 inches
FLOWER COLOR: pink buds; white
mature flowers
BLOOM TIME: July to August
LIGHT: sun or part-shade
PROPAGATION: seed or division
   Meadowsweet is great for wild
gardens, but adapts well to
cultivated sites as well.
   Seed can be obtained from
plantsmen who specialize in
wildflowers. Or, you may be able to
locate a friend who will give you a
clump to start in your own garden. It
multiplies rapidly and can be lifted,
divided, and replanted every few years
until you have the supply you want.
   One of meadowsweet's values is
that it can help fill in a period when
many hardy perennials have ended
their season. Too, it's very
undemanding as to soil, though it
does require moisture if it is to
bloom well.
   Clusters of double flowers are
carried on straight stems arising
from rosettes of fern-like foliage.
   As often happens with common
plant names, there is another plant
also called meadowsweet to which
filipendula is unrelated. It is of the
rose family, *Spiraea latifolia,* and is
of shrub-like habit, with plumes of

fragrant pink flowers in summer.
You may find it in the woods from
Newfoundland as far south as
Virginia. But don't dig it up, as it is an
endangered species.

MERTENSIA
see Virginia bluebells

MONARDA
see bee-balm

MONKSHOOD
(*Aconitum* sp.)

ZONE: 3 **HEIGHT:** 3 to 5 feet
FLOWER COLOR: blue, purple-
blue, yellow, white
BLOOM TIME: July, August,
September
LIGHT: sun or light-shade
PROPAGATION: seed or root
division
   Because they bloom in late
summer and fill a void before the
chrysanthemums come into flower,
monkshood finds a welcome in
many perennial borders.
   The plant needs a constant supply
of moisture, but rejects any location
where water stands. Be sure to
choose a well-drained planting site.

Barker's variety, which grows to 4 feet in height, is perfect at the back of the border and its blue-purple bloom contrasts in striking fashion with many of the yellow daylilies that are in bloom during the same late-summer period.

Aconitum carmichaeli (formerly known as *A. wilsoni*) grows to 5 feet tall and puts up big spikes of rich blue flowers. It's also an excellent daylily companion.

Golden Yellow Monkshood, to 3 feet, combines well with clumps of white or purple phlox.

Seed should be sown in late summer, with seedling plants set into a cold frame for the winter and moved to the garden when frost danger has passed. These plants usually bloom the second season.

Roots of all varieties are poisonous and care should be taken not to plant them where children or animals can get to them.

MULLEIN
see verbascum

O

OBEDIENCE
see physostegia

OENOTHERA
(*Oenothera* sp.); also called sundrops and evening primrose

ZONE: 3 or 4, depending on variety
HEIGHT: 12 to 18 inches
FLOWER COLOR: golden yellow
BLOOM TIME: June through August
LIGHT: full sun
PROPAGATION: seed or root division

The hardiest of the species and the most often cultivated in perennial borders is the variety Highlight (zone 3). Very free-flowering, it displays flat trusses of cup-shaped bloom and is most effective when it is grown in good-sized groups.

Oenothera fruticosa's flowers are a somewhat paler yellow, and it forms an 18-inch plant (zone 4).

O. missourensis, just 12 inches tall, has blooms that measure up to 4 inches in diameter, and is hardy from zone 4 southward.

All varieties need well-drained soil, on the sandy side, but enriched before planting with well-rotted manure. Set out new plants 8 inches apart in spring or fall.

P-Q

PAINTED DAISY
(*Chrysanthemum coccineum*); also known as pyrethrum

ZONE: 4   **HEIGHT:** 14 to 24 in.
FLOWER COLOR: white, pink, and red
BLOOM TIME: June-July
LIGHT: sun
PROPAGATION: root division or seed

This member of the chrysanthemum family blooms in

June, about the same time as the bearded iris.

Its fern-like foliage and colorful bloom make it a useful mixed perennial border plant, grown in a mid-border placement. Allow about a foot between plants. Each clump will spread, and in two to three years you can lift, divide, and replant to increase your supply. The best time to divide is late-summer.

To start new plants, sow seed in spring, or set out root starts purchased from the nursery. Both single and double forms are available in nursery starts.

Painted daisies need a rich soil and ample moisture. If your soil is poor, prepare the bed by spading in compost, leaf mold, or well-rotted cow manure. Water the location thoroughly and let stand for several days before setting in new plants.

PAPAVER

see poppy

PENSTEMON

(*Penstemon* sp.)

ZONE: 3 to 5, depending on variety
HEIGHT: 12 to 20 inches
FLOWER COLOR: blue, purple, red, rose
BLOOM TIME: June-July
LIGHT: sun or light-shade
PROPAGATION: seed or root division

The spiky growth habit of this attractive perennial makes it a useful plant to give variety to a border containing many rounded-form plants—such as daisies, bee-balm, helenium, and gaillardia.

Flowers are reminiscent in shape of foxglove, with many blooms on each stem, and are good as cutting flowers as well as in the border.

One recommended variety, Firebird, has ruby-color blooms on 18- to 24-inch stems. It's easy to grow, free from pests, and free-flowering. Zone 5.

Penstemon newberryi is somewhat shorter—12-inch stems—with rose-purple bloom in June. Prune it back after the first flowering and you'll almost certainly have a second crop of flowers at summer's end. Zone 5.

An extra-hardy (zone 3) variety, Rose Elf grows 18 to 20 inches tall, with flowers of a clear rose color blooming freely from June until the arrival of frost.

If drainage is good and plants have ample water during the summer months, the penstemons are an easily grown perennial, with a long period of bloom. Plant in the spring or in the fall, spacing 10 inches apart.

PEONY

(*Paeonia* sp.)

ZONE: 3 **HEIGHT:** 18 to 30 inches
FLOWER COLOR: white, range of reds, pinks, yellows occurring in tree peony group
BLOOM TIME: May-June
LIGHT: sun or part-sun
PROPAGATION: root division in fall for herbaceous types

Double herbaceous peonies are a major event of early summer in almost every part of our country. Huge blooms and attractive green foliage that remains good-looking when bloom has disappeared are their endearing qualities. So are their resistance to virtually all pests, their long-life qualities, and their ability to withstand periods of drought in hot summers. Their range of colors and forms (see pages 10 and 11 for illustrations of several varieties) puts peonies in the almost-indispensable group of perennials for most flower gardeners.

Well-planted (see pages 10 and 11), your peonies will require almost no attention from you other than working some fertilizer into the soil around each plant when its season of bloom is over. You may leave plants undisturbed for a great many years—up to twenty. Or, if you wish more of the same kind, you can divide and replant about once every six to ten years.

In addition to the double peony which is best known, there are attractive singles, Japanese, and semi-double varieties. And there is also the less-widely-known tree peony, so called because, unlike the herbaceous types just listed, its woody branches do not die down to the ground in winter. At maturity, tree peonies grow up to 6 feet tall and may bear as many as 80 blooms—a truly striking sight in a spring garden.

Among the herbaceous peonies, there are early-, mid-, and late-season blooming varieties. Choose some of each to prolong the time you can enjoy these flowers in the garden and in magnificent bouquets. Many are quite fragrant.

Fall is the best time to set out new peony plants. See that they are watered well and regularly until frost hardens the soil. Then put on a protective layer of mulch, using straw, hay, or clippings from your evergreens. It will not be necessary to continue this winter protection after the first year.

In its first spring, a peony plant may sometimes show signs of wilt that is fungus-produced. In such cases, fungicide sprays will control the problem. Cut off and burn any affected stalks. This measure will not be necessary in following years, once the plant has become established and produces sturdier shoots in spring.

If you are anxious to produce the largest possible bloom, you'll want to "disbud" bloom stalks by cutting off side shoots. It will be necessary to supply some support for these heavy-headed beauties, so stake all outside stems to prevent them from toppling over in heavy wind or rain.

Don't allow seed heads to form. When flowers shatter, clip away the entire flower head. And, after the first killing frost, cut off dead foliage and remove all weeds that encircle the plants.

Tree peonies

Never make the mistake of cutting down woody stems of a tree peony as you would the leafy stems of the herbaceous varieties. If you do, you may find yourself with no tree peony the following spring, but instead, an herbaceous peony (tree peonies are grafted to the more hardy herbaceous peony root stock). After a few years, the herbaceous peony roots wither away and the tree peony's roots become firmly established.

After the initial planting of a tree peony in fall, be sure to keep it well-watered until frost. Then cover with an upside-down bushel basket weighted to stay in place through winter months. This protective measure need not be taken in following years.

In spring, after the second year, work a pound of bone meal into the topsoil surrounding each plant, taking care not to dig so deeply as to damage shallow roots.

Tree peonies bloom slightly ahead of herbaceous peonies each year, and remain handsome shrubs for the rest of the season until frost causes leaves to fall. As with herbaceous peonies, clip off the entire heads when blooms shatter. Do not allow to go to seed.

Recommended varieties

The immense popularity of peonies makes them the subject of continuing crossbreeding by a number of growers. And when a new variety is produced and put on the market, it is certain to carry a high price tag for a few years, until quantities available are large enough to meet demand.

But unless you become a peony fancier, there is no need to spend much per plant to have a wide variety of beautiful and time-tested varieties for your garden. For less than five dollars, you may expect field-grown plants that have from three to five "eyes," ready to bloom the spring after planting. (Your plant will increase in size more rapidly if you do not cut stems of the first year's bloom; cut sparingly from crops for the next year or two.)

Single and Japanese varieties are mostly mid-season bloomers, except for hybrids which are all early.

In the white-cream list, Bu-Te, Krinkled White, and Pico are all popular; pink Barrington Belle and Sea Shell rank high; and red Hari-Ai-Nin and White Cap top the lists. Among hybrids of these categories, choose Sprite (white), Flame (pink), and Burma Ruby, or Scarlett O'Hara (red) for early season bloom.

Semi-doubles that head many favorite lists are: Miss America (white), Liebschen (pink), and the

Mighty Mo and Hoosierland (reds). Hybrids in this class, blooming a bit earlier (mid-season) than those just listed, include these sure-to-please varieties: Coral Charm and Paula Fay (pinks); and Carina and Red Glory (reds).

Doubles, probably the most popular of all herbaceous peonies, include these top-sellers: Moon River, Bowl of Cream, Festiva Maxima (white-blush-creams); Dolorodell, Mrs. F. D. Roosevelt, Dinner Plate, First Lady (early) and Pink Jazz (pinks); and Jay Cee and Cherry Hill (reds). Of these, Cherry Hill is early, and Jay Cee is a mid-season bloomer.

Tree Peonies will cost more to buy than herbaceous kinds because they involve the labor of grafting scions onto herbaceous roots.

Among the American hybrid varieties that sell most widely are these choice plants: Black Pirate (dark red), Coronal (ivory blushed with rose), Golden Hind (clear yellow bloom, maroon flares), High Noon (lemon yellow), Princess (mauve), Redon (pink), Renown (copper red), and Vesuvian (dark red, fully double). All of these tree peonies are reliably hardy in zone 4, and with protection, in zone 3.

Japanese tree peony hybrids that top popularity lists include: Fuson No Tsukasa and Godaishy (whites); Yachiyo Tsubaki and Hanakisoi (pinks); Higurashi and Taiyo (reds); and Kamata Fugi and Rimpo (purples). Of the yellow tree peony hybrids, Alice Harding is probably the universally favorite variety.

PHLOX
(*Phlox* sp.)

ZONE: 4 **HEIGHT:** to 4 feet
FLOWER COLOR: white, pinks, reds, lavenders, purples
BLOOM TIME: July until frost
LIGHT: sun, part-sun
PROPAGATION: root division

For fragrance, magnificent trusses of colorful bloom that are very long-lasting, and ease of culture, the perennial hardy phlox is deservedly popular.

A major factor in growing phlox successfully is advance preparation of the bed. Soil should be deeply spaded and enriched with bone meal or other organic plant food. Plants should be set at least 1 foot apart and kept well-drained. Spacing is especially important if you are to avoid the one pest phlox are subject to: mold on foliage. While it will not kill the plant, mold is certainly unsightly. But if air circulates freely, the danger of mold is minimal.

Keep plants thinned out so that each supports no more than four or five stalks. Divide roots about every three years, and clip off bloom heads before they go to seed. Plants from such seed will not be true (most will be unlovely shades of lavender), and if any of these appear, pull and destroy them. The best time to divide and replant is early spring.

The most important work in hybrid phlox development has been done by the late Captain Symons-Jeune. Many varieties created by him have brilliant "eyes" that contrast nicely with the main color of the florets: pink centers on white florets, red centers on pink florets, etc.

In mixed perennial borders, set phlox at back-of-border positions and use them as accompaniments to daylilies, tall hardy asters, or rudbeckia. Phlox, somewhat like lilies, prefer to have their "feet" in the shade, but their "heads" in the sun, so a mulch is helpful. When watering, always use a soaker hose or other method of keeping water on the soil, rather than spraying from above. This helps control mold.

Recommended whites include: Iceberg (white with red eye), White Admiral, and Mount Fujiyama. Outstanding lavender-through-purple phlox are: Lilac Time, Russian Violet, and Royalty. In the pink-through-red group, these are favorites: B. Symons-Jeune (rose pink with crimson eye), Fairy's Petticoat (pale pink with deep pink eye), Dodo Hanbury Forbes (clear pink), Prince Charming (flame red), Windsor (rose red), Starfire (brilliant red), and Othello (clear red).

A rarity in the phlox tribe is the dwarf Pinafore Pink, which seldom reaches a height of more than 6 inches. Use it at the front of the border for a novel effect.

PHYSALIS
see Chinese-lantern

PHYSOSTEGIA
(*Physostegia* sp.); also called false dragonhead or obedience plant

ZONE: 3 **HEIGHT:** to 2½ feet
FLOWER COLOR: white, pink
BLOOM TIME: July to September
LIGHT: sun
PROPAGATION: root division
The wildflower *Physostegia virginiana* has been hybridized by plantsmen and is a good addition to perennial borders. Flowers are carried on tall spikes or branching racemes and will remind you in their form of foxglove (digitalis).

Most attractive grown in groups, individual plants should be spaced 12 inches apart. Roots will spread quite rapidly and may be divided every two years. New plants may be set out in either spring or fall.

P. virginiana Vivid is about 20 inches tall, and has flowers of a fine, deep pink. Grow it at mid-border position alongside Shasta daisies or other flowers of round form for a pleasing contrast.

Summer Snow, as its name suggests, puts out pure white bloom on 2½-foot stems. It may be used at mid- or back-border positions in mixed perennial borders, or is handsome grown in large clumps by itself.

PINCUSHION FLOWER
see scabiosa

PINKS
see dianthus

PLANTAIN LILY
see hosta

PLATYCODON
see balloon flower

PLUMBAGO
see leadwort

POLEMONIUM
see Jacob's-ladder

POKER PLANT
(*Kniphofia* sp.); also called torch lily

ZONE: 5   **HEIGHT:** 3 to 5 feet
FLOWER COLOR: white, pastels, vivid yellows, reds
BLOOM TIME: spring through summer
LIGHT: sun or part-sun
PROPAGATION: root division

For this South African native, hybridizers have developed a number of good varieties which are reasonably hardy, but which will require winter mulching in the northern zones.

Flower stalks rise up from grass-like mounds of foliage with many drooping blooms on the terminal end, forming a poker-like cluster from which the plant takes its common name.

When the period of flowering ends, cut away flower spikes, and cut old leaves to an inch or so above the ground in the fall. New foliage will come up in the spring.

Set new plants which have fleshy roots into a sunny, well-drained location in the spring, and allow 18 inches of space between them.

POPPY
(*Papaver orientale*)

ZONE: 2   **HEIGHT:** 2 to 4 feet
FLOWER COLOR: red, white, pink, orange, lavender
BLOOM TIME: early summer
LIGHT: full sun
PROPAGATION: root division

Today's Oriental poppies—hybrids developed from varieties that grow wild in Mediterranean countries—are eye-dazzling in both size and color range. Flower heads often measure 6 to 8 inches across with soft, gleaming petals reminiscent of the finest silk cloth.

Whatever the flower color, it is often enhanced by the sharp contrast of near-black splotches at the base of petals.

Easy to please where soil is concerned, they perform most handsomely in rich loam. New plants must be set out in August or September when plants are dormant. Try to place where you'll want permanent growth, for poppies deeply resent moves. Place the crown 2 or 3 inches below the surrounding soil level and space plants 15 to 18 inches apart. Keep well-watered till frost hardens the ground. In the first season, supply a mulch for winter protection or mound soil over the plant's crown. This step will be unnecessary in following years.

Just don't expect bountiful bloom the first spring after planting Oriental poppies. It takes them a while to get "settled in." But in years thereafter, you should be amply rewarded for your patience by these "show-offs" of the perennial world.

Choose a sunny and well-drained location for poppies. If possible, place them behind plants (such as daylilies) whose foliage will hide poppy foliage as it ripens, then gradually withers away following the bloom season.

Recommended varieties

Barr's White is universally chosen as an outstanding poppy, and is most striking planted alongside a strong red such as Glowing Embers or Surprise. Good pinks are Helen Elizabeth and Lighthouse. Rosy varieties you'll like include Curlilocks, Salome, and the well-named Watermelon.

In the coral-to-orange range, try Tangerine, Pandora (8-inch bloom!), or Bonfire. Lavender Glory (lavender is a less-common color among Oriental poppies) is dramatic with three large basal splotches of black.

The Iceland poppy is a close relative of the Oriental species. For information on this plant, see Iceland poppy.

PYRETHRUM
see painted daisy

POTENTILLA

(*Potentilla* sp.); also known as cinquefoil

ZONE: 4-5 **HEIGHT:** 3 to 18 inches
FLOWER COLOR: yellow, cerise, orange
BLOOM TIME: June to frost
LIGHT: sun or part-sun
PROPAGATION: root division

In its short varieties, potentilla is very useful as an edging for a mixed border, or to grow in a rock garden. Cinquefoil, its other name, derives from the fact that leaves are "five-fingered." The plant form resembles that of creeping wild strawberries. Natives in the northern zones of the United States, they are hardy and will grow readily in any type of soil. Blooms resemble wild roses, but on a smaller scale.

Potentilla aurea puts on most of its color show with a profusion of small yellow flowers in May and June. It's only 3 inches tall, Zone 4.

P. nepalensis Miss Willmott grows to 1 foot in height, with cerise bloom all summer. Zone 4.

Lady Rolleston, 18 inches tall, bears 1½- to 2-inch bloom of orange-gold hue from June to September. It's hardy from zone 5 south. *P. verna* is a low-growing creeper with mat like foliage.

PRIMROSE

(*Primula* sp.)

ZONE: 3, 4, or 5, depending on variety
HEIGHT: to 12 inches
FLOWER COLOR: white, pink, blue, red, gold, mixed
BLOOM TIME: early spring
LIGHT: shade or part-shade
PROPAGATION: seed or root division

The primrose family, a very large one, includes a few that are relatively easy to grow if you can provide them with the right location and climatic conditions. All demand soils rich in peat, whether natural or a supplement, and ample moisture. When you set out new plants, allow 4 to 6 inches of space between each.

The polyanthus strain is apt to be the one you'll prefer because of its relatively large bloom borne on 9-inch stems. Bloom colors of the polyanthus variety are brilliant pinks, reds, yellows, scarlets, and purples, as well as white. They are usually offered in mixtures, as exact colors are difficult to guarantee (zone 3).

Primula vulgaris, the true English primrose, has creamy-yellow flowers with a deeper yellow eye on 4- to 5-inch stems. It's well-suited to the rock garden or as an edging for a shady mixed border (zone 5).

P. denticulata produces bloom in the lavender-to-purple range and has stems as tall as 12 inches. It's hardy from zone 4 south.

P. Japonica Millar's Crimson has candelabra-like bloom arranged in whorls around the stalk. Individual blooms are 1 inch in width, with stems as tall as 2 feet (zone 5).

Premier variety has exceptional bloom—up to 3 inches across in a wide range of colors (zone 5).

All members of the primrose group are subject to red spider. To control this pest, flush plants thoroughly with water as soon as hot weather begins, and continue to do so periodically throughout the summer. Once a plant is infected, it's hard to cure.

R

RUDBEKIA

(*Rudbekia* sp.); also known as coneflower

ZONE: 3 **HEIGHT:** to 30 inches
FLOWER COLOR: yellow-gold
BLOOM TIME: July until frost
LIGHT: sun or part-sun
PROPAGATION: root division

Close relatives of the black- or brown-eyed susan (a biennial), there are two cultivated varieties of the coneflower that can and should be grown in almost any mixed

59

perennial border. They are Gold Drop and Goldsturm, both of which grow easily and compactly, and produce large golden-yellow bloom during a period when few other perennials are flowering. Gold Drop is double; Goldsturm, single.

Both withstand heat and drought well, and neither is subject to damage by insect or disease. They flower most freely in full sun, but will tolerate a surprising amount of shade and still put out a good supply of bloom.

Fall's the time to set out new plants, or to lift and divide.

S

SALVIA

(*Salvia* sp.); also known as sage

ZONE: 4   **HEIGHT:** to 3 feet
FLOWER COLOR: blue, blue-violet, red
BLOOM TIME: summer to autumn
LIGHT: sun
PROPAGATION: division
    Perennial plants with blue flowers that bloom mid- or late-summer are not easy to find, but blue sage is one

that meets these specifications. Flowers are borne on spikes or racemes, and spent stems should be regularly cut away to keep the plant blooming steadily.

Any average garden soil will suit these plants, and they spread quite rapidly. Set out new plants in early spring, spacing them 10 inches apart, then divide and replant every three years.

The variety East Friesland produces 18-inch flower spikes in June and continues to bloom all summer. Flowers are an intense hue of violet-tinged blue, and are good to cut for indoor use.

The Pitcher's sage displays gentian blue flowers borne on a shrubby plant that grows as tall as 3 feet. This variety, grown in zone 4, will require a protected location and winter mulch.

The cooking herb, *S. officinalis*, can be grown from seed or root starts purchased from a nursery. But scarlet sage, *Salvia splendens*, takes on shrubby characteristics and so isn't used as often in the perennial border.

SANTOLINA

(*Santolina chamaecyparissus*); also called lavender cotton

ZONE: 6   **HEIGHT:** to 2 feet
FLOWER COLOR: yellow
BLOOM SEASON: June-July
LIGHT: sun
PROPAGATION: division
    Several varieties of this small shrub-like plant are grown mainly for their attractive aromatic foliage (reminiscent of lavender), as edgings for mixed borders, as low hedges, or in rock gardens. Several varieties have feathery foliage of a silvery hue that makes a pleasing contrast with the bright flower colors in a mixed border.

Santolinas aren't winter-hardy north of zone 6, but some northern gardeners grow plants in pots and keep them in a cold frame for the winter. They also lend themselves to growing as bonsai and can be wintered over as a houseplant in a sunny window.

Santolinas bloom in June and July, with yellow button-like flowers. Plants should be pruned after the

flowering period ends.

You may plant either in spring or fall, spacing plants 6 inches apart in sandy soil and full sun.

Recommended varieties include Nana, that will reach a height of 8 inches but should be kept pruned to 6 when used as a miniature hedge of silvery gray; Neapolitana, also silver-leaved with graceful pendulous branches; and *Santolina virens*, with dark evergreen foliage, which will tolerate poor soil and hot summer sun.

SCABIOSA

(*Scabiosa* sp.); also known as pincushion flower

ZONE: 5   **HEIGHT:** to 30 inches
FLOWER COLOR: white, blue, lavender
BLOOM TIME: summer
LIGHT: sun
PROPAGATION: seed or root division
    Named for its protruding white stamens above a cushion-like bloom—giving the appearance of pins stuck into a pincushion—this plant is effective in mixed borders and makes an excellent cut flower.

Both giant and dwarf strains are obtainable—the dwarfs reaching a height of 18 inches; the giants, 2½ feet.

Seed may be sown in fall and carried through the winter in a cold frame, ready to set into the open garden as soon as frost danger has passed. These seedlings will bloom in early summer.

Spring-planted seed may bloom by late summer of the first year after planting. Seeds of both the dwarf and giant types are sold in mixed, rather than individual, colors.

SEDUM
(*Sedum* sp.); also called stonecrop

ZONE: 3 **HEIGHT:** dwarf to 2 feet
FLOWER COLOR: orange, yellow, red, pink, cream, white, rust-brown
BLOOM TIME: spring or late summer
LIGHT: sun
PROPAGATION: root division

The sedums, fleshy-leaved plants equipped for storing up water and so able to withstand periods of drought, serve many useful garden purposes: in rockeries, as edgings for borders, and—for a few—as good border plants themselves.

Most bloom in summer, but there also are a few spring-blooming sedums. Some have colorful foliage even when not in bloom.

Spring is the best time to set out new plants, and they should be spaced 12 to 15 inches apart, as most varieties increase rapidly.

Sedum kamtschaticum is one of the most dramatic varieties, sending up many bright orange clusters of bloom from July on. When autumn arrives, the rich, dark green foliage becomes red and gold. Its height of 3 to 4 inches makes it suitable as an edging for a border, or to plant in rock gardens.

S. kamtschaticum variegatum has all the same growth patterns as the previous variety, but its foliage carries a band of white. Plant alternating clumps of these two for an attractive pattern.

The floriferum form of *S. kamtschaticum* comes originally from Siberia, and is especially hardy. Never growing to more than 6 inches, the plant is covered with golden-yellow bloom during July and August. Use it as a border edging or in a rock garden.

S. telephium Indian Chief, a plant that is from 10 to 14 inches tall, has gray-green foliage, with each stem topped in early autumn by an umbel of copper-colored bloom. Each plant produces 10 or more bloom stems, making this variety a good choice for perennial borders.

S. Maximum atropurpureum is often called the mahogany plant because of its foliage color. Creamy rose blooms appear in August. Use it in flower arrangements as well as in the mixed perennial border. It's from 18 to 24 inches in height.

S. sieboldi has plump, silvery gray foliage, and in early September, bright pink bloom on 6- to 9-inch stems. Variegatum, the variegated form of *S. sieboldi* just described, has foliage that is sprinkled with cream-colored spots.

S. spectabile Meteor grows to 18 inches tall. Foliage is gray-green, with flowers appearing in umbels of red in summer. It's effective in mixed borders and in bouquets.

The Star Dust form of spectabile has blue-green leaves and puts up big flower heads of ivory bloom in late summer. It's 18 inches tall.

S. spathulifolium Capa Blanca, an English import, is a low-growing, slow-spreading sedum with blue-green foliage in rosettes. Bright yellow bloom appears in May or early June.

S. Spurium Dragon's Blood is one of the dwarfs—an inch or two tall—that remains in bloom from July to September. The foliage takes on the tints of deciduous trees in autumn.

SHASTA DAISY
(*Chrysanthemum maximum* or *C. x superbum*)

ZONE: 4 **HEIGHT:** 2 to 3 feet
FLOWER COLOR: white with yellow centers
BLOOM TIME: early summer
LIGHT: sun, part-sun
PROPAGATION: seed or root division

61

Among the many varieties of shasta daisy, you'll find both singles and doubles that will be outstanding in a mixed perennial border. They are not, however, reliably winter-hardy and will need winter protection in zone 4.

Set new plants a foot apart in rich soil, mulching around the base to retain moisture. If you start from seed, sow in spring.

Every other spring, you should lift, divide, and replant divisions to keep plants healthy. Under good growing conditions, bloom can be 3 to 4 inches across, excellent for cutting as well as for border display. Variety Alaska is a good single; Marconi, a recommended double shasta.

SNOW-IN-SUMMER
see cerastium

SOLIDAGO
(*Solidago* sp.); also called hybrid goldenrod

ZONE: 3   **HEIGHT:** to 3 feet
FLOWER COLOR: rich gold
BLOOM TIME: August-September
LIGHT: sun or part-sun
PROPAGATION: root divisions

If you're one who thinks of this stately plant as a weed, think again. It has been falsely accused of causing hay fever, but it is ragweed pollen—its timetable coinciding closely with goldenrod—that is the villain. If you've visited the majestic herbaceous borders maintained by many of the colleges of Oxford, you've seen it dramatically used and much admired.

Consider planting it at the back of a mixed border in clumps that alternate with hardy asters in purple hues. They make a stunning combination when both are in bloom.

The Golden Mosa variety is a strong branching plant with tapered bloom trusses of deep yellow-gold. It's about 3 feet tall.

SPEEDWELL
see veronica

SPURGE
(*Euphorbia* sp.)

ZONE: 4   **HEIGHT:** 12 to 15 inches
FLOWER COLOR: yellow
BLOOM TIME: April-May
LIGHT: sun or part-sun
PROPAGATION: root division

The euphorbias are most often used in rock gardens, but they are also good accent plants for mixed borders. They thrive in hot, dry sunny spots that would kill off many perennials.

Euphorbia epithymoides, sometimes called milkwort (all plants of this genus have a sticky,

milky fluid in their veins), is bushy in form, grows 12 to 15 inches tall, and puts out yellow bracts of bloom in May. As summer progresses, these change to a rosy-bronze, but foliage remains deep green throughout the season. Although it spreads readily, you can keep it where you wish if you pull up any unwanted plants in the spring. This is also a good time for separating and replanting clumps if you want to increase your stock of this and other euphorbias.

Milkwort is a formal-looking plant that works well in the border or rock garden.

E. myrsinites, cushion spurge, is a prostrate plant that has stiff blue-green foliage growing in spiral whorls about the stems. Heads of yellow bloom appear in April and May. Use it in rock gardens and as a ground cover in hot, dry, and sunny locations.

STACHYS
(*Stachys* sp.); also known as lambs-ears or betony

ZONE: 4   **HEIGHT:** 8 to 12 inches
FLOWER COLOR: red
BLOOM TIME: summer
LIGHT: sun or part-sun
PROPAGATION: root division

Often seen in old-fashioned gardens, stachys has been increasing in popularity in recent years because of its ease of care, willingness to grow in poor soil, and effective contrast of color and texture in the mixed perennial flower border.

Its common name is an accurate description of its soft, furry foliage; the bloom is insignificant.

The inviting, woolly-white leaves of *Stachys byzantina* reach a height of about 8 inches. A taller variety, *S. olympica*, matures at 10 to 12 inches and has leaves that are 6 to 8 inches long. Red flowers rise 10 to 12 inches above foliage when the plant is in bloom.

STOKESIA
(*Stokesia laevis*); also known as Stokes' aster

ZONE: 5 **HEIGHT:** 12 to 15 inches
FLOWER COLOR: light blue or white
BLOOM TIME: July into September
LIGHT: sun
PROPAGATION: root division

A valuable midsummer-into-autumn bloomer in the perennial garden, stokesia is quite undemanding except for sun and good drainage. It may be planted either in early spring or autumn, but leave 6 inches of space between each plant.

Blue Danube is the most commonly grown stokesia. Its light blue flowers, which can be up to 5 inches in diameter, may remind you more of bachelors' buttons than of asters. Place this one toward the front of a mixed border.

Silver Moon stokesia is a hybrid of Blue Danube with the same growth habits. Big white flowers are tinged with blue-to-lavender at the center of the bloom.

SUNDROPS
see oenothera

SWEET WILLIAM
see dianthus

T-U

THALICTRUM
(*Thalictrum* sp.); also known as meadow rue

ZONE: 3 **HEIGHT:** 3 to 4 feet
FLOWER COLOR: yellow, white, lavender
BLOOM TIME: June-July
LIGHT: shade, part-shade
PROPAGATION: seed or root division

The graceful foliage of thalictrum is similar to that of columbines, and there are several varieties to choose from if you're willing to grow these plants from seed. Only *Thalictrum minus* is widely offered as a plant by growers. It blooms in July with fragrant heads of green-tinged yellow bloom. All meadow rues are good in perennial borders that are partly shaded.

T. polygamum, tall meadow rue, is 5 to 7 feet tall, bears white bloom in panicles, and blooms from July onward. It requires winter protection if grown north of zone 4.

T. rochenbrunianum, lavender mist meadow rue, is only 3 feet tall, has lavender bloom with yellow stamens, and blooms from May to September.

T. speciosissimum (glaucum), dusty meadow rue, has frothy yellow

bloom heads in summer. Hardy from zone 5 southward, it grows 3 to 4 feet tall.

To obtain seed of the various meadow rues described here, secure catalogs from plantsmen who are specialists in wildflowers. Some of these wildflower specialists also sell field-grown plants.

If you do grow from seed, the best time to sow is late summer; transfer seedlings to a cold frame for the winter, and set into the open garden in early spring. All varieties should bloom that season.

Seed sown in early spring probably will not bloom until the next garden season.

THERMOPSIS
(*Thermopsis caroliniana*); also known as Carolina lupine

ZONE: 3 **HEIGHT:** 3 to 4 feet
FLOWER COLOR: yellow
BLOOM TIME: June-July
LIGHT: sun
PROPAGATION: root division or seed

Although there are a good many plants in the genus, only the one described here, Carolina lupine, is widely offered for sale by plantsmen.

63

The plant has graceful form, attractive dark green leaves, and sends up spikes of sweet pea-like bloom in midsummer.

For climates where summers are often hot and dry, this is a plant to count on—unlike the true lupines which cannot tolerate spells of hot, dry weather.

Set out new plants or divisions in either early spring or autumn. Or, sow seed in early fall. Space plants 18 inches apart.

THRIFT

(*Armeria maritima*); also called sea thrift and sea pink

ZONE: 3 **HEIGHT:** dwarf
FLOWER COLOR: rose, white
BLOOM TIME: May to July
LIGHT: full sun
PROPAGATION: root division

This appealing family of small hardy perennials is most often used in rock gardens. Although certainly effective in such placements, it also lends itself well to use as an edging plant for a mixed perennial border. It's attractive all season.

Its major requirements are full sun and a well-drained site, but it is not at all fussy about soil type.

New plants may be set out in the spring or autumn, about 8 or 10 inches apart. Each will soon form a tidy mound of foliage from which flower stems arise.

The white form of *Armeria maritima* sends up many 5-inch bloom stems in the form of tufts of very narrow leaves that rise above its low mat of dark green foliage.

A. laucheana is 6 inches tall and bears many vivid rosy heads of bloom in May and June. Foliage is evergreen.

Royal Rose, a hybrid developed from the variety just described, puts up 15-inch flower stems bearing pink globe-shaped blooms.

TRANSVAAL DAISY
see *gerbera*

TROLLIUS
see globeflower

V-W-X

VERBASCUM

(*Verbascum* sp.); also called mullein

ZONE: 5 **HEIGHT:** 30 inches to 6 feet
FLOWER COLOR: yellow, white, pink, salmon, violet
BLOOM TIME: June to October
LIGHT: full sun
PROPAGATION: root division

For those hot, dry spots unfriendly to many perennials, try verbascum. Furry gray foliage makes this an interesting contrast plant in a mixed border. And tall forms make good back-border subjects. Just give it plenty of sun and a well-drained location to get good performance.

Verbascum phoeniceum comes in mixed colors—white, pink, salmon, and violet—blooming from June until October. It grows from 3 to 6 feet tall, depending on how well the planting location suits its needs, and is hardy from zone 6 southward.

Pink Domino, 4 feet tall, has pink flowers with maroon eyes.

VERONICA

(*Veronica* sp.); also known as speedwell

ZONE: 3   **HEIGHT:** 6 to 36 inches
FLOWER COLOR: shades of blue, white, pink
BLOOM TIME: June to September
LIGHT: sun
PROPAGATION: root division

This large genus includes both shrub and perennial plants, but shrub forms are hardy only in the warmest zones of our country.

Among the perennial plants, there is a good range of sizes, suiting some for use in rock gardens or as low edgings for borders, and others for placement at mid- or back-of-the-border.

All varieties should have bloom stems cut off as soon as flowers fade to encourage a longer season of

bloom. Once planted, veronica should not be moved. But if a move is unavoidable, do it in early autumn and keep the plant well-watered until the ground freezes.

Veronica alpina alba puts on a show of white bloom that continues all summer if spent bloom stalks are faithfully removed and not allowed to go to seed. It's just 6 inches tall, and so is ideal for use in rock gardens, or as an edging for a mixed perennial border.

Spikes of bloom of the Barcarole variety are rose-pink in color, and the plant, 10 inches tall. Flowers keep coming from June until late August if spent bloom is cut.

Crater Lake Blue is a free-flowering variety that's at its best in early summer. Colorful spikes of deep sky blue bloom grow on sturdy 18-inch stems.

Blue Giantess bears deep blue flowers on spikes that can reach 3½ feet in height, while the Rosea variety, just 1½ feet tall, has bloom spikes of a rosy pink. Icicle is a pure white, has 18-inch flower spikes, and is a good cut flower.

VIOLA

(*Viola* sp.)

ZONE: 3 to 5, depending on variety
HEIGHT: 4 to 6 inches
FLOWER COLOR: blue, purple, pink, white
BLOOM TIME: early spring
LIGHT: part-shade
PROPAGATION: root division

Violas are relatives of pansies, but are a good deal easier to keep perennial. There are two major groups within the genus: sweet (*Viola idorata*) and tufted (*V. cornuta*). Both want good garden loam which has been enriched with leaf mold, well-rotted manure, or peat. Soil must be moist, though it should have good drainage.

However, even if you can meet these conditions in spring, violas aren't for you if your area is accustomed to long, hot, dry summers. In that case, you may have to grow them from seed and replant when you lose plants to adverse weather conditions.

To grow violas from seed, sow in late summer, transplant seedlings to a cold frame for the winter, and, for bloom that season, set out into garden location as early as the ground can be worked. Space plants 10 to 12 inches apart.

Seed sown in early spring will probably bloom that fall. Many viola varieties will produce a smaller fall crop every year if weather conditions are right: enough rain and no early spell of frost.

In the *Viola odorata* group, Rosina produces generous amounts of fragrant pink bloom on 8-inch stems. Zone 3.

Red Giant, with fragrant long-stemmed, red-violet flowers, develops into a good-sized clump quite rapidly, with leaves larger than most violas. Zone 4.

Royal Robe has violet-blue bloom on 6-inch stems. This variety can take somewhat more sun than can most other violas. Zone 4.

White Czar, like Royal Robe, is also tolerant of part-sun locations and has big flowers on 6-inch stems. Zone 4.

In the cornuta group, the variety Catherine Sharp is a very desirable plant. It produces generous amounts of bloom over long periods, and plants rapidly increase in size. By the second year, a clump may measure a whopping 24 inches across. Zone 3.

Floraire is one of the earliest to bloom, its lavender-blue flowers touched with darker splotches of color. If summers are cool, it may continue to bloom for the entire season. Zone 3.

Purple Glory has deep velvety-purple bloom with a yellow eye. Bloom stems are from 5 to 8 inches long, and plants are hardy from zone 3 southward.

Jersey Gem Alba is a white variety of similar growth habits to Purple Glory. Zone 3.

VIRGINIA BLUEBELLS
(Mertensia virginica)

ZONE: 3   **HEIGHT:** 18 to 24 inches
FLOWER COLOR: blue
BLOOM TIME: early spring
LIGHT: shade, part-shade
PROPAGATION: root division

Lovely companions to the spring-flowering bulbs, clumps of Virginia bluebells are easy to grow, make no special demands about soil type, and prefer light shade.

Although they're especially handsome when naturalized on a grassy slope, you must be prepared to leave the area unmowed until foliage yellows and dies back.

Mertensia virginica has tubular shaped flowers of sky-blue color on 18- to 24-inch stems that sway in spring breezes. Flowers turn pink as they open fully and mature.

YARROW
(Achillea sp.)

ZONE: 3   **HEIGHT:** 6 inches to 3 feet
FLOWER COLOR: white, red, yellow
BLOOM TIME: June to September
LIGHT: sun or part-sun
PROPAGATION: root division

Most varieties of achillea are on the tall side—2 to 3 feet—though there are also varieties that are mat-like, with flowers borne on 4- to 6-inch stems. Some are excellent to cut, dry, and use in fall bouquets, with Coronation Gold one that's especially suited to this use. Fern-like foliage is typical of the achillea varieties.

These plants perform well in dry locations and are not fussy about soil, but do best in good loam.

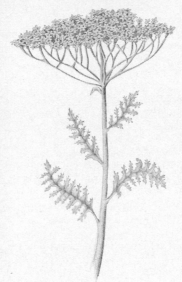

Achillea ageratifolia, a low-growing variety, is well-suited to use in rock gardens or as an edging for borders. Single, daisy-like bloom on 4- to 6-inch stems begins in June and goes on until September. This variety needs alkaline soil; if yours is acidic, have a sample analyzed and add the correct amount of lime to sweeten it.

Coronation Gold, already cited as good for drying, grows to 3 feet and is in bloom from June to August.

A. millefolium Fire King, as its name suggests, has rosy-red flower heads on 24-inch stems. Foliage is a silver-gray in color.

A. ptarmica Angel's Breath looks like a larger-size variety of baby's-breath, its white rosettes of bloom in clusters at the tips of 18-inch stems. The plant is bushy in habit.

A. filipendulina Moonshine produces canary-yellow bloom on umbels on 18- to 24-inch stems. It's in bloom from June to September, and foliage is silver-gray color.

YUCCA
(Yucca sp.)

ZONE: 4   **HEIGHT:** 3 to 6 feet
FLOWER COLOR: creamy white
BLOOM TIME: summer
LIGHT: sun
PROPAGATION: root division

Striking all season long because of its sword-like ball of pointed foliage, yuccas put on their show of bloom in spectacular fashion, sending up bloom spikes that can be as tall as 6 feet, with half their length covered by creamy-white, bell-shaped flowers.

For a hot, dry, sunny location, the yucca is one of the best suited plants. It demands good drainage, but little else in the way of care.

Yucca filamentosa has evergreen foliage, and puts up flower spikes that are at least 3 feet in height.

Y. filamentosa Bright Edge, a newer variegated form, carries a band of gold edging on its deep green spiky leaves. Use this one for accent in a doorway planting where there's sun and well-drained soil.

Y. flaccida Ivory Tower is the most spectacular of the varieties listed here, with bloom spikes which may be as tall as 5 or 6 feet and are laden with creamy-white flowers that grow upright, rather than pendant.

Gas plant, in both white and pink varieties, blooms all summer long.

Perennial Know-How

Hardy perennials that flower for brief or lengthy periods are desirable garden plants no matter where you grow them. But in a mixed border, they're absolutely indispensable.

If you're just starting your perennial border, you'll almost certainly rely on some annuals to fill bare spots during part of the season. But if you plan well, you'll eventually have a handsome mixed border of all perennials.

To achieve this, draw up a plan (see following pages). Make lists of those varieties best suited to the conditions of soil and light you can offer, and then buy or grow from seed the perennials you need to fill the border space available. Keep heights and colors in mind as you plant.

CHOOSE PERENNIALS BY HEIGHT

Front-of-the-Border (Dwarf to 15 inches)	Mid-Border (15 to 30 inches)	Back-of-the-Border (Over 30 inches)
Anemone (*Anemone canadensis*)	Allium (bulb)	Anchusa (variety Dropmore)
Aster (dwarf Michaelmas varieties)	Astilbe	Aster, hardy (Michaelmas daisies)
Baby's-breath (*Gypsophila repens*)	Baby's-breath (gypsophila)	Baptisia (false indigo)
Bellflower (*Campanula carpatica*)	Balloon flower (platycodon)	Coneflower (rudbeckia)
Bugloss (anchusa)	Bee-balm (monarda)	Delphinium (species varieties)
Candytuft (iberis)	Bleeding heart (dicentra)	Daylily (hemerocallis)
Chrysanthemum (cushion varieties)	Butterfly weed (*Asclepias tuberosa*)	Foxglove (some varieties such as Excelsior hybrids)*
Cinquefoil (potentilla)	Chrysanthemum (many varieties)	Globe thistle (echinops)
Cranesbill geranium	Columbine (aquilegia)	Goldenrod (solidago)
Crocus (bulb)	Coreopsis	Helenium
Dwarf iris varieties	Coral bells (heuchera)	Heliopsis
English daisy (bellis)*	Delphinium	Heliotrope (centranthus)
Feverfew	Gaillardia	Hollyhock (*Alcea rosea*)*
Flax (linum)	Gas plant (dictamnus)	Hibiscus
Grape hyacinth (bulb)	Iris	Iris (spuria and Japanese)
Hyacinth (bulb)	Foxglove (digitalis)*	Liatris (gayfeather)
Lavender	Lilies (many varieties)	Lilies (many hybrid varieties)
Narcissi (miniature varieties; bulbs)	Lobelia	Lupine
Painted daisy (pyrethrum)	Loosestrife (lythrum)	Mullein (verbascum)
Pinks (dianthus)	Peony	Phlox
Phlox (*Phlox subulata*)	Poppy (papaver)	Sunflower (helianthus)
Plumbago (dwarf)	Phlox	Thermopsis (Carolina lupine)
Primrose (primula)	Rudbeckia	Yarrow (achillea, variety Coronation Gold)
Salvia, perennial blue sage	Shasta daisy	Yucca
Silver Mound (artemisia)	Spiderwort (tradescantia)	
Stokesia (Stoke's aster)	Tulips	*Biennial
Tulip (botanical varieties; bulb)	Virginia bluebells (mertensia)	
Veronica (some varieties)		
Viola		

You're already doing something to increase your perennial know-how: reading a book. But also study seed and plant catalogs and garden columns in your local newspaper. Some are extremely well-done, with accurate information on zonal hardiness and culture for many varieties. And, if you're lucky enough to live near a large nursery of perennial plants, by all means pay a visit (check first to learn the days and hours when the public is invited to tour).

It's also a good idea to write your own garden book—in the form of a diary. Note in it the varieties planted (whether seed or plants), and the time of planting. Follow up with notes on time of bloom, temperature lows and highs, flower color, health problems, and a record of the rainfall.

Be sure to keep an accurate chart of where you've set plants, and mark with a name-stake all that emerge late, whose foliage disappears from view after blooming. This could prevent losing a plant by digging into a spot that appears—deceptively—to be bare.

APPROXIMATE BLOOM DATES

Spring	Summer	Fall
February through early May	*Mid-May through August*	*Late August to Frost*

Spring	Summer	Fall
Alkanet (anchusa)	Astilbe	Aster, hardy (Michaelmas daisy)
Anemone canadensis	Baby's-breath (gypsophila)	Christmas rose
Artemisia Silver Mound	Balloon flower (platycodon)	Chrysanthemum
Basket-of-gold alyssum	Bellflower (campanula)	Candytuft (iberis variety
Crocus (bulb)	Bee-balm (monarda)	Autumn Snow)
Bleeding heart	Butterfly weed *(Asclepias tuberosa)*	Daylilies (hemerocallis) late-season varieties
Dwarf iris	Columbine (aquilegia)	Dianthus (Allwoodi "alpinus")
Grape hyacinth (muscari; bulb)	Coreopsis	Sedum
Hyacinth (bulb)	Coral bells (heuchera)	Tradescantia (Blue Stone)
Iberis (candytuft)	Daylily (hemerocallis)	
Phlox subulata	Delphinium	
Scilla siberica (bulb)	Gaillardia	
Tulip (botanical varieties; bulb)	Gayfeather (liatris)	
Viola	Gas plant (dictamnus)	
Virginia bluebells (mertensia)	Globe thistle (echinops)	
	Heliopsis	
	Helenium	
	Iris	
	Lilies (bulb)	
	Lobelia	
	Loosestrife (lythrum)	
	Peony	
	Poppy (papaver)	
	Phlox	
	Rudbekia	
	Salvia (perennial blue sage)	
	Shasta daisy	
	Spiderwort (tradescantia)	
	Thermopsis (Carolina lupine)	
	Veronica	
	Yarrow	

Note: Many of the "summer" perennials will continue to bloom until frost if dead bloom is regularly removed and the plant is not allowed to go to seed earlier in the season. A few of the early varieties, such as viola, may well have a second season of bloom if the fall is cool and the moisture supply is sufficient.

Perennial Know-How

Once you've decided on the kinds of perennials you'll grow in your border, it's time to make a placement chart. Though some will be short, some mid-height, and others tall, all will look best if they're planted according to height—preferably in groups of at least three per variety.

If possible, install a backdrop for the show in the form of a hedge, fence, or garden wall. This will also protect against strong winds, and will help keep plants from toppling in a sudden storm. And, it's good protection from wintry blasts even when the garden's not in bloom.

SUNNY PERENNIAL BORDER

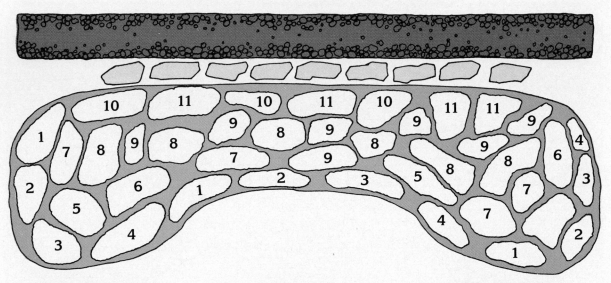

Front-of-the-Border
1. crocus
2. species tulips
3. iberis snowflake
4. basket-of-gold alyssum

Mid-Border
5. hyacinth
6. tulip (Plant early and late varieties to lengthen the season.)
7. narcissus
8. daylilies (hemerocallis) (In this spot, choose varieties under 30 inches.)
9. iris (Include bearded, spuria, Siberian, and Japanese varieties.)

Back-of-the-Border
10. delphinium (Choose tall, large-flowering kinds such as Pacific Coast hybrids, Blackmore, Langdon, and Bishop.)
11. lilies (Choose Pacific hybrid varieties.)

Note: Depending on your color scheme, such annuals as zinnias and marigolds, or geraniums and coleus could be set into areas where bulb foliage has yellowed and ripened off, leaving unattractive bare spots for much of the summer season. Note, also, that daylilies have been purposefully positioned so that their foliage will emerge slowly, ready to cover some of the spots made bare by ripened-off bulb foliage. Stepping-stones placed between the border and background hedge help make cultivation easier.

Unless your border's narrower than 3 feet, it's important to allow for reaching plants from either back or front—for planting, weeding, fertilizing and so on. Stepping-stones of natural flagstone, or a brick path are two practical solutions. If you pour pea gravel between stones and along the path, you'll avoid awkward weeding. Lay plastic under stones to inhibit weeds.

Note that the sunny border is planned for 25 feet in length, and the shady border for 10. If you'd like yours either longer or shorter, simply repeat or decrease plant groupings to fit the desired length of bed.

In both garden plans, the lists of plants are only suggestions. For each one, there are a number of others that would work equally well. See the charts on these two pages, and the earlier section, "ABCs of Perennials," for helpful alternate selections.

PART-SHADE PERENNIAL BORDER

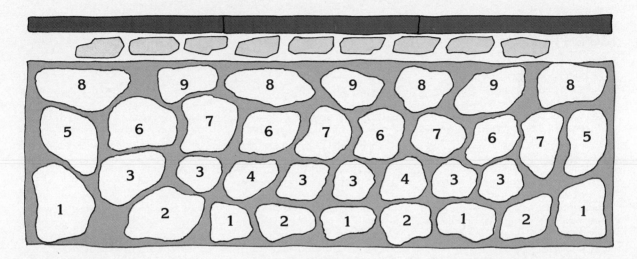

Front-of-the-Border
1. hardy cyclamen (or small-leaf hosta, such as *Hosta lancifolia*)
2. primrose (primula)
3. astilbe
4. bleeding heart *(Dicentra spectabilis)*

Mid-Border
5. hosta (large leaf varieties such as *Hosta fortunei* or *Hosta seiboldiana*)
6. Siberian iris (available in a range of blues, whites, and purples)
7. globe flower (trollius)

Back-of-the-Border
8. false indigo *(baptisia australis)*
9. loosestrife (lythrum variety Morden's Gleam)

Note: "Part-shade" here means that the location receives morning and perhaps late afternoon sun, but not midday sun. If shade is not too dense, daylilies are an excellent choice for back-of-the-border plantings; they will not bloom as heavily as in full sun, but will give an adequate performance. The Goldsturm rudbeckia is also a good mid-border alternate choice, as it, too, blooms satisfactorily if shade's not too dense. Stepping-stones placed between the border and the background fence make for easier cultivation.

Perennial Know-How

Some nurseries and garden stores sell perennials already growing in containers. In both fall and spring, perennials are also available as dormant, bare-root plants. You can plant dormant roots with very little risk of loss. In northern zones, fall-planted roots start growing at the normal time in the spring.

SOIL PREPARATION

Whether you're planting perennials in a bed, border, or other area, always prepare the soil thoroughly before you plant. The best soil lies near the surface. So if you must remove sod, strip off the top layer, trying not to take off more than an inch of soil.

Locate all perennial plants at least 3 feet from any tree or shrub so they won't have to compete with massive roots. Use a spading fork to remove grass and weak roots, as illustrated above. Spade the soil well, turning it over to a depth of 8 to 10 inches. Then rake the soil to level it, removing all stones and breaking up clods. Use the fork to work in a 2- to 4-inch layer of peat moss or well-rotted cow manure. (*Exception:* Omit manure in preparing bulb beds.) Organic matter improves the soil structure and provides better growing conditions for all plants.

It's wise when preparing a large bed to take the steps outlined above in the fall. Then leave the area unplanted until spring so winter rains and snows have time to mix in all additives and the soil can naturally settle into place.

If your soil has an overly high clay content—heavy, sticky, and hard to work—you should fork in coarse sand and fine gravel as well as peat until you have a lighter mix. Vermiculite or perlite can also be used to good advantage to lighten this type of garden soil.

If you move into a fairly new home and discover that the builder has put a very thin layer of topsoil over clay, your best bet is to tackle the problem at once, before you attempt any planting. Decide on the place or places where you want perennial beds and remove at least 3 feet of poor soil in those areas. Have loads of black dirt brought in to replace soil removed.

If this sounds like a drastic step, remember that it will certainly be easier to do now than later. And it could make all the difference between a good and a poor future garden.

PLANTING

It's difficult to generalize about planting perennials because each is quite individual. However, here are some steps to help ensure success. First, set the plants at the proper depth—at the same level they grew the previous season. You can see marks of the former depth on the dormant roots you buy. Next, provide adequate space for roots so they're not crowded. Dig a hole several inches larger in diameter than the width of the roots and spread roots out so they can quickly get established. It often helps to build up a low cone of earth at the bottom of the hole so you can easily space roots out over the cone. Then, gradually sprinkle in soil.

Remember that your main goal in transplanting—whether new plants or those you obtain through division of your older plants—is to avoid shocking plants. Don't let roots dry out or break off. They're the plant's lifeline to food, moisture, and good health.

Choose a day to plant that is cool, cloudy, or even a bit rainy. If it's warm or sunny, keep plant roots shaded and covered with layers of water-soaked newspaper until you're ready to plant. Lift plants gently and set at the same level at which they formerly grew.

Gradually fill in earth about the roots and firm the soil to eliminate all air pockets. Water thoroughly immediately after transplanting and continue to water every day until soaking rains make certain the new plants are settled in.

If you plant in the fall, mark the location of new plants. Some are quite late to emerge in spring, and you can easily forget their location if it's unstaked. Cover them with a light mulch for the winter, then remove it in the spring as plants first appear. But keep some mulch handy in case a late frost should make it advisable to re-cover the young, tender shoots.

Don't use raked leaves as mulch. Winter snows and rains turn them into a soggy mass that doesn't perform the most important function of mulch: not to keep plants warmer, but to prevent the soil from heaving when rapid

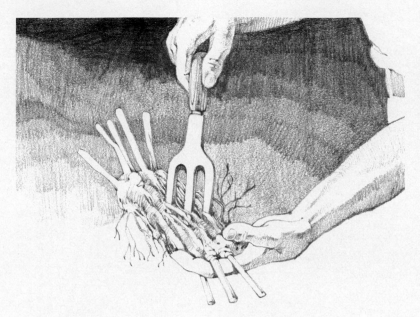

temperature changes cause freezing and thawing.

Much better materials to use for winter mulch are straw, hay, or pruned branches of evergreens. If you haven't enough evergreens for the entire job, use what you have as a top layer. The greens will improve the appearance of the mulch and help hold it in place.

DIVIDING

You can divide some perennial roots by gently tearing off sections. In the case of tuberous or woody roots, it's best to use a hand fork or a sharp knife. Don't try to make too many divisions out of one plant, and be sure each division has adequate roots to sustain it while it's recovering from the shock of division. In the case of peonies, be sure to have at least three "eyes" on each division, or you'll wait a long time before you have bloom from them. Five-eye divisions will often bloom the first season after you divide.

When dividing any plants, it's a good idea to wash soil away from the roots so you can see what you're doing. Direct the hose stream away from the base of the stems to avoid bud injury. Keep as many roots attached to each division as possible, but trim away any damaged roots. If any part of the division looks dead or diseased,

trim all the way back to clean, white tissue. Replant as soon as possible after dividing any perennials.

Shown above is the correct use of a hand fork to divide roots of such perennials as hemerocallis.

WINTER PROTECTION

In addition to the general mulch previously described, there are other ways to cut down on losses of plants to winter freezes. Several of them are described and illustrated below. None takes much time or costly equipment, but each may save you the loss of a valued plant.

Put a protective covering over small tufts of fall growth. An inverted flowerpot over a madonna lily keeps mulch from packing around the new shoot.

If you live in an area where winter temperatures frequently fall below freezing and often remain at low levels for prolonged periods of time, you will have to protect all beds of perennial plants with a general layer of mulch, as has been described. The best time to mulch for complete plant protection is as soon as possible after the first killing frost. (This is usually preceded in cold climates by one or more "light" frosts which nip the tops but do not kill plant foliage back to the ground.)

Before you put on mulch, clear the beds of all dead foliage and weeds, cutting stems of plants back to within 2 inches of the soil; then add fertilizer, such as bone meal or a general garden fertilizer.

For perennial beds exposed to wind, here's an easy way to keep mulch in place. Lay on sections of poultry wire weighted down at intervals with bricks or stones.

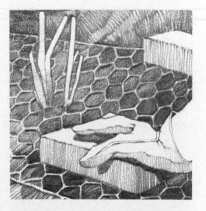

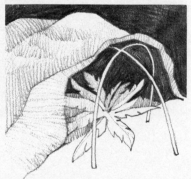

Make a frame of crossed wire loops to protect fall growth of Oriental poppies. Cover with burlap and pile soil on edges to hold in place.

73

Hardy Bulbs

For all who live in a cold wintry climate, few spring sights can excel the first colorful appearance of bright crocus. Coming along a bit later to splash clear blue on a barren garden bed are scillas and grape hyacinths.

Monarchs of the spring bulb parade are tulips and daffodils which hybridizers have developed in a breathtaking variety. Tulips are available in early-, mid-, and late-season types to help prolong the bulb season well into May.

The hardy bulb family also counts glory-of-the-snow, bulb iris, snowdrop (galanthus), and Roman or wood hyacinth among its spring array. And then there are the relatives, such as lily-of-the-valley, grown from "pips," and eranthis, grown from corms, to add to spring color and fragrance.

All spring-flowering bulbs (and relatives) must be planted in the fall. Most are rather easygoing about the soil type, but all need good drainage, so avoid low spots.

A good rule of thumb about planting depth for various bulbs is that it should equal three times the diameter of the bulb. So tiny bulbs, like crocus, need to be planted only 2 to 3 inches deep. A hyacinth bulb will need a hole 8 to 10 inches deep.

The best fertilizer for hardy bulbs is bone meal, and some should be added to the soil when planting.

With the exception of standard tulips, all spring-flowering hardy bulbs listed here may be "naturalized"—or grown in grass, on hillsides, under trees, and allowed to multiply naturally each year. But such plantings **must** stay unmowed until bulb foliage yellows. This allows the bulb to build up

strength for bloom the next spring. Easily suited to natural plantings are most varieties of narcissus or daffodils (daffodils are, in fact, members of the narcissus family). Avoid bulbs of questionable hardiness in your growing zone if you're planning to naturalize.

If you live in zone 9 southward, you will have to treat tulips as annual plants, for they need a long dormant period of cold weather in order to bloom in spring. But it would be a shame to miss the show entirely, and southern gardeners can purchase cold-treated bulbs or may do their own cold-treating by refrigerating bulbs for at least 6 weeks at 40° F. Plant bulbs after the first of December for spring bloom.

In addition to their uses in beds and borders, many hardy bulbs are fine subjects for forcing (bringing into bloom weeks ahead of outdoor flowering dates, to be enjoyed indoors).

Hyacinths and narcissus are the easiest, but if you pick the right varieties, there are many tulips that force very well.

Rules for forcing all bulbs are to plant bulbs in pots in the fall; place where temperatures of 40 to 45° F. will be maintained for approximately 12 weeks (in bottom of refrigerator, in root cellar, or in an outdoor trench). Soil must be kept fairly moist during this time, but not so wet that rot occurs.

If you choose to set pots into an

outdoor trench, dig it 18 inches deep and line it with hay or straw, tucking some in between pots as you set them in place. Cover tops of pots with more straw or hay; then add soil and leaves to reach soil level.

In January, check to see if good roots have formed. If so, bring indoors to a cool, dark place until the foliage is up from 4 to 5 inches. Then bring into warmth and strong light to watch flower buds shoot up.

If you choose to force tulips, the single early and darwin classes are easiest. Among single earlies, try Bellona (golden-yellow), Coleur Cardinal (crimson), or Princess Irene (salmon). Good darwins, include Apeldoorn (orange-scarlet, black base) and Paul Richter (red).

How to Use Bulbs

A massed planting of hardy spring-flowering bulbs is by far the most spectacular way to use them—even if there are no more than 20 or 30 bulbs in the "mass." It will heighten the visual impact to use all one variety and color in a group. Mixing colors and kinds tends to give a patchwork look. In a mixed border, space bulbs among the perennials that will bloom later, counting on perennial foliage to hide ripening bulb foliage. Plant at least five to a group.

For a cool green-white scene, set White Triumphator tulips (lily-flowered) next to white azaleas and a green box hedge.

Trumpet daffodil Unsurpassable, above, produces collosal flowers of gold-yellow, and is easy to force (see forcing instructions on page 75). Pots decorate brick ledges flanking a garden fountain and pool. Berlioz, below, of the kaufmanniana group, teams well with daffodil Jack Snipe. Star magnolia, right, backs narcissus Mrs. Ernst H. Krelage.

HARDY BULBS

Tulips

Tulips form such a varied and gorgeous tribe that they deserve your study. Consult bulb catalogs and get to know the species or botanical tulips—they're closer to being perennial than the darwin or cottage types. Included in this group are fosteriana, greigi, and kaufmanniana tulips.

Bunch-flowered tulips, as their name implies, send up several blooms on a branched stem. In the May-flowering group are cottage and darwins. Others you should know include graceful lily-flowered, parrot (Gay Presto, above, is one of the parrot group), peony, and fringed tulips.

Remember that all tulips must have excellent drainage and full sun in spring. Let foliage ripen naturally, helping bulbs to bloom the next spring.

Kaufmanniana tulips bloom early on stems 4 to 8 inches long.

Tall stems and cup-shaped blooms are typical of darwin tulips.

For late bloom on very tall stems, plant cottage tulips.

HARDY BULBS

Daffodils

Grow narcissus (daffodils) for many years of spring pleasure. Mostly hardy from zone 4 south, they self-propagate to make big clumps of small ones in a few years' time. To encourage spreading, plant 5 to 7 inches deep in a well-drained location. Plant in fall.

The wide variety of forms in which this bulb is available includes: flatcup, poeticus, trumpet, miniatures, triandrus or bunch-flowered, split-cup (shown above), and cyclamen-flowered.

Remarkably good for naturalizing are trumpet variety narcissus.

Cyclamineus narcissus.

Triandrus narcissus are among the late-flowering varieties.

81

HARDY BULBS
Other Favorites

Earliest spring color is the gift of the little hardy bulbs, like the vivid blue, 6-inch grape-hyacinths above. Muscari (their botanical name) thrive in sun or shade.

There is also a white variety of muscari. Both will multiply rapidly over the years and are a good choice for naturalizing. They bloom in early March. Zone 4.

Eranthus or winter aconite sends up yellow flowers on 5-inch stems in February. It likes shade and a moist location.

Chionodoxa or glory-of-the-snow: starry blue or pink flowers with white centers. Blooms in March, in sun or shade.

Hyacinths White Carnegie, Pink Pearl, and King of the Blues

Hardy through zone 5.
Anemone blanda *shows its 6- to 9-inch blue or rose daisy-like blooms in March; it is a handsome companion for early daffodils. Soak bulbs in water overnight, then plant in shade. Most varieties not hardy north of zone 6.*

Galanthus, or snowdrop, puts up a nodding white bell-shaped bloom before frost goes out. Plant 3 inches deep and 3 inches apart in light shade.

Inexpensive to buy, they multiply quickly. Zone 4.

Puschkinia: creamy white flowers touched with blue. Blooms March and April; sun or shade. Flower stems 8 to 12 inches. Plant 3 inches deep. Zone 4.

Hyacinths for Scent

Hyacinths can perfume the air of your spring bulb garden, besides adding their colors of blue-purple, rose-pink, white, and yellow.

Larger than the bulbs

we've been discussing previously on these pages, hyacinths need to be planted deeper—about 8 inches. Be sure planting site is well drained.

Besides their outdoor uses, hyacinths are easy to force. Buy top-size bulbs, and see instructions for forcing on page 75. Good varieties for forcing include Jan Bos (red), Lady Derby (pink), Bismark (blue), Perle Brillante (blue), Carnegie (white), and L'Innocence (white).

83

Allium giganteum *puts up huge ball-like blooms on 5-foot stems.*

Chrysantha tulip, 8 inches tall. March.

Six-inch hoop-petticoat narcissus. March.

Little-known bulbs could easily join your list of favorites if you choose those hardy to your zone and suited to your soil. Some are tiny, some huge; some bloom in spring, others in summer, and a few in autumn.

Across the page are pictured three bulb plants you may never have grown. All would make excellent additions to your mixed perennial border, or could be grown in beds of their own.

Related to Allium giganteum *and also blooming in summer, is* A. christophi; *its ball of bloom less dense and bearing lavender star-shaped flowers on a 2-foot stem. It, too, is June-flowering. Zone 4.*

Camassia, *which thrives in sun or shade, sends up tall bloom spikes that produce hundreds of blue-purple, star-shaped flowers; May. Zone 4.*

Dogtooth violet, *or* Erythronium, *is probably better called by its other, less-widely-used common name—trout lily. Some varieties, such as E. multiscapoideum, bloom early and are more heat- and drought-resistant than the native trout lily—E. americanum. All varieties have slim, mottled foliage, and most have yellow flowers with recurved petals. Plant in* light shade. May bloom. Zones 4 through 8.

Snowflake, *or* Leucojum aestivum, *puts up tall scapes, 8 to 10 inches, bearing a white bloom that is reminiscent of lily-of-the-valley, much enlarged, and with green dots at the tips of the scalloped edges. Blooms April through May. Plant in fall, 4 inches deep and the same distance apart. Snowflake prefers rich, sandy soil, and is effective in plantings coupled with* chionodoxa. *Zone 4.*

Summer and Fall Bloom

Although it is true that most of the hardy bulbs bloom in spring, there are a few—in addition to the alliums and hardy lilies already discussed—that are of interest for summer-fall bloom.

Eremurus, *fox-tail lily or desert-candle, actually grows from a corm rather than a bulb. Hardy through zone 5. It will need a heavy winter mulch when grown farther north. In June, flower scapes growing as high as 8 feet arise from low-growing foliage rosettes. Flowers are borne on half the length of the stem and stay in bloom for weeks. Foliage disappears after bloom period; may be over-planted with annuals. Shelford hybrids of this* plant reach only 3 to 4 feet, and come in mixed hues of pink, orange, yellow, cream, and rose.

Hardy cyclamen *is from 4 to 6 inches tall, with attractive foliage that, on a miniature scale, closely resembles the potted greenhouse specimens we associate with Christmas. Most varieties bloom in fall—early September.* Cyclamen purpurascens *has crimson flowers in autumn. Hardy in zone 6, and in zone 5, if protected.*

Lycoris, *or spider-lily, a member of the amaryllis family, sends up strap-shaped foliage in spring. This dies and disappears. Then fragrant pink lily-like blooms on 2-foot stems appear in August.* Lycoris squamigera *should be planted 8 inches deep in part-shade. Reliably hardy in zones 4 through 9.*

Colchicum *bulbs come on the market in late summer and should be planted immediately. The big vase-shape lavender bloom appears within weeks after planting. The next year dense foliage appears in the spring. This ripens slowly, so choose a location where other foliage will disguise the unsightly leaves. Plant a foot deep in part-shade. Bulbs multiply rapidly. Zone 4.*

Bulb Know-How

Spring-flowering bulbs must be planted in autumn, before deep frost hardens the ground. Once in the earth, roots begin to grow and flowers start to form inside the bulbs, continuing even when heavy snows come and temperatures plummet. In northern gardens and in Canada, planting times range from September to November. In southern states, planting time will begin a month or so later.

In the deep South, where no true winter occurs, tulips and hyacinths must be treated as annuals—they will not bloom the following year. And the bulbs—if not already cold-treated—must be pre-cooled before planting. Do this by storing bulbs in the bottom of your refrigerator at 40° to 50° F. for 6 to 12 weeks.

Flowering times vary depending on season (early or late), placement of bed (plants facing south flower earlier), shade or sun (tulips in part-shade flower later), and other environmental factors.

Be sure the site you've selected is well-drained, for if water stands, bulbs will rot. In soil with too much clay, use peat and vermiculite to lighten the consistency. Work bone meal into the soil at the bottom of the hole or bed where you'll plant the bulbs, and topdress with balanced fertilizer after blooming. Do *not* cut off foliage, but allow it to ripen naturally. You should, however, clip off all flower stems as soon as bloom is spent.

If any amount of time elapses between purchase and planting of tulips, be sure to store bulbs in a dark, cool place—temperatures not over 70° F. And if you plant on a warm, sunny day, *never* leave bulbs in the sun. Even a short time under such conditions will noticeably reduce the size of bloom.

Field mice are a menace to newly planted tulips in some areas. To reduce such danger, don't plant bulbs next to garden walls or house foundations where mice make runs. And before planting, clean beds of all garden waste that could make ideal mice nests.

For your convenience in planting bulbs near each other which will bloom at about the same time, use the following chart. It also lists height at maturity, depth to plant, and space to allow between bulbs.

A GUIDE TO BULB CULTURE

Flowering Period	Genus and Species or Variety	Average Height at Maturity (Inches)	Depth of Planting (Inches)	Space Between Bulbs (Inches)
Very Early *March 15-30*	Crocus chrysanthus	3-4	4	2-3
	Crocus sieberi	3-4	4	2-3
	Crocus tomasinianus	3-4	4	3-4
	Eranthis species	3-4	4	2-3
	Galanthus species	3-4	4	2-3
	Iris reticulata	4-5	4	2-3
	Scilla tubergeniana	4-6	4	3-4
Early *March 31-April 20*	Anemone blanda	3-4	4	2
	Chionodoxa species	5-8	4	2-3
	Crocus flavus	3-4	4	3-4
	Crocus vernus	4-6	4	3-4
	Muscari azureum	4-5	4	1-2
	Narcissus cyclamineus	10-14	6	4-6
	Puschkini scilloides	4-6	4	3-4
	Scilla siberica	4-6	4	3-4

Flowering Period	Genus and Species or Variety	Average Height at Maturity (Inches)	Depth of Planting (Inches)	Space Between Bulbs (Inches)
Mid-Spring April 21-May 15	Erythronium 'Pagoda'	8-12	4	3-4
	Fritillaria imperialis	25-30	6	8
	Fritillaria meleagris	6-8	4	3-4
	Muscari armeniacum	6-8	4	4
	Muscari botryoides album	4-5	4	1-2
	Narcissus jonquilla	10-14	6	3-4
	Narcissus triandrus Thalia	10-14	6	4-6
	Narcissus W. P. Milner	8-10	6	4-5
	Hyacinth Blue Jacket	10-12	6	9
Late May 16-June 5	Allium aflatunense	26-30	4	4
	*Allium elatum	32-40	6	6
	Allium karataviense	8-10	4	6-8
	*Allium rosenbachianum	40-48	6	6
	*Camassia quamash	12-16	6	4
	*Ixiolirion tataricum	15-17	4	6
	Narcissus Baby Moon	10-14	6	4-5
	Ornithogalum umbellatum	8-10	4	3-4
Very Late June 6-July 1	*Allium caeruleum	20-26	4	2-3
	Allium christophi	20-26	4	6-8
	Allium giganteum	40-48	6	6
	Allium moly	10-14	4	2-3
	Allium oreophilum	10-14	4	2-3
	Allium sphaerocephalon	22-26	4	3-4
	*Triteleia laxa	12-16	4	4

*Not reliably winter-hardy north of zone 5.

TIPS ON PLANTING TULIP VARIETIES ACCORDING TO SEASON OF BLOOM

For earliest spring tulip bloom, choose the botanical or species types. These include the fosteriana, greigi, and kaufmanniana types, as well as Tulipa clusiana, T. praestans (variety Praestans Fusilier), and T. pulchella (variety Violacea). This last-named variety will bloom with late crocus; all others can be expected to bloom in mid-April with narcissus. The botanicals also have the virtue of being more nearly perennial than the more hybridized varieties such as the cottage, darwin, and parrot tulips. Most of the botanicals are close to the tulips that first sent Hollanders into the frenzy called "tulipomania" when early travelers brought home bulbs from Turkey. Today, native varieties are imported from Russia to cross with others in a never-ending search for something new.

The enormously popular tall darwin tulips which bloom in May are followed by the cottage tulips.

The darwin hybrids, including such well-known varieties as Parade, Oxford, Gudoshnik, and Apeldoorn, are the result of crossing darwins with Red Emperor, and can be counted on to bloom about a week ahead of the darwins.

Darwins such as The Bishop (violet with a blue throat), Queen of the Bartigons (salmon-pink), Balalaika (red), and Glacier (white), bloom slightly later in May than do the cottage tulips: Halcro (red), Mrs. J. T. Scheepers (yellow), Spring Snow (white), and Blushing Bride (yellow and rose).

Bulb Know-How

Tulips, hyacinths, and the other spring-flowering bulbs must all be planted in the fall. Depth of planting is related to the size of the bulb, as the chart below shows.

SOIL PREPARATION

Dig soil for all bulbs to full spade depth. If soil is heavy, turn under a thick layer of compost to improve drainage. For bulb beds, it's also wise to spade in a fertilizer high in phosphorus and potash at the same time, such as 3-18-18. Level and rake smooth.

Proper tillage can go a long way toward improving the structure of your soil. On the other hand, improper tillage can do your soil great harm.

Never till your soil when it's too wet. If you can take a handful of soil and squeeze it together to form a sticky, compact mass, then it's too wet to be worked. Heavy clay soils that are tilled when they're too wet become hard and lumpy.

But even when the moisture content is right, it's possible to overwork your soil. Avoid working it so finely that it will crust after a rain. Instead, try to break up the clods and level the surface without destroying the structure of the soil.

PLANTING

For a bed of several types of bulbs, outline the area for each group with the end of a rake handle. Space tulips and other big bulbs fairly close (5 or 6 inches) to make a splashy color effect (wide spacing weakens their impact). Set bulbs inside outlines before you plant, and print varietal names on stakes set at the center of each group. Plunge garden trowel full depth, as shown above; pull toward you to open pocket; and set bulb firmly in place. Then cover with soil. Very deep planting of tulips (10 to 12 inches) inhibits offset formations that weaken main bulbs.

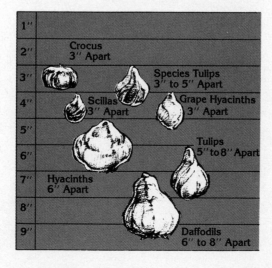

Use the chart at left to determine proper planting depth for a wide variety of spring-flowering bulbs. Also note recommended distances for spacing them.

88

REPLANTING

Although digging up tulips after blooming is not recommended, it can be done. However, it's best to leave the bulb in place during the period when foliage is yellowing and dying down. It is in this period that the bulb makes the most use of strength gained through foliage

to help form bloom for the following season.

If tulips must be dug before foliage ripens, dig a shallow trench and heel-in bulbs with foliage attached. Mark the variety, and lift later to replace in a permanent garden location.

MAINTENANCE

In addition to applying plant food to tulips when you plant them, you also should add it immediately after the blooming period ends. Water beds liberally during every drought, but try to keep water from getting on the leaves; hose-soak the root areas. A 2-inch layer of good mulch, such as cocoa bean hulls, straw, or ground corncobs, will conserve soil moisture and will also help keep down weeds.

Always snap off seed heads when bloom fades. The plant's energy will

then go into the formation of larger bulbs for the next season of bloom. Flower stems may be left standing.

Even though you plant fine bulbs and give them good care, you'll find that the hybrid tulips tend to throw smaller bloom after a few years, and finally disappear except, perhaps, for a few shoots of foliage. Species or botanicals, however, are much more nearly perennial by nature. This group includes the fosteriana, the greigi, and the kaufmanniana groups—all well worth exploring. Most bloom on fairly short stems, and many bloom considerably earlier than do the hybrid varieties.

MICE PROTECTION

Mice and chipmunks can be a real source of trouble if you plant bulbs in quantities. The only sure way to protect newly planted bulbs against this kind of damage is to place them in baskets fashioned from hardware cloth, their tops left open. This technique, unfortunately, is too time-consuming and expensive except in smaller gardens.

NATURALIZING BULBS

Hybrid tulip varieties are not good subjects for "naturalizing"—that is, planting on slopes, in grass, or under trees to give the effect of natural growth.

Narcissus are among the showiest and most satisfactory of bulbs to grow in this manner, and many growers offer either a mixture of bulbs just for this purpose, or greatly reduced prices on varieties purchased in large quantities—by the thousand. These bulbs produce bulblets that, left undisturbed, will eventually form a clump of blooming narcissus where you originally planted a single bulb.

To gain the natural look, some gardeners favor standing still and casting a handful of bulbs into the air, letting them fall where they will, then using a trowel to make an appropriately deep hole for each bulb where it lies. For the same effect sooner, plant bulbs in groups of three, fairly widely spaced.

Don't avoid planting in areas under trees. The early spring-blooming bulbs will have bloomed and their foliage will have ripened in the sun that comes through branches of deciduous trees at this season. In fact, blooms will last longer and retain a deeper color in a planting site covered by light shade during the warmest part of the day. The one area to avoid in naturalizing—or, for that matter, in planting any bulbs—is one that constantly stays wet or moist. Bulbs will rot if roots are kept wet.

WINTER PROTECTION

Applying several inches of mulch over perennial beds that include spring-flowering bulbs is a wise precaution in areas where sudden thaws and freezes might cause the ground to heave, damaging bulbs and roots. The best materials are those that let rain and melting snow come through easily, keeping moisture levels adequate. Straw, hay, and the prunings from evergreens are best.

As important as applying the mulch either just before or just after a killing frost is knowing when to remove it. Left in place too long, it will damage tender foliage shoots when you take it off. Taken off too soon, it renders plants vulnerable to a sudden frost that could nip and "brown" tips of leaves, as well as flower buds.

Since the arrival of spring varies widely from area to area—and even from week to week within the same area in different years—the safest way to decide when to lift mulch is to make frequent checks as weather begins to warm. Usually when tulip foliage is 2 inches above soil, it's time to take off the mulch.

DISEASES AND PESTS

Quality bulbs are subject to few pests or diseases. But if a plant should show signs of disease, such as misshapen foliage, it's wise to lift and destroy the entire plant so that the disease will not spread. Healthy bulbs should feel firm and solid to the touch; don't plant those that seem soft or spongy. If you buy your bulbs through reliable dealers, you probably needn't worry about diseases or their treatment.

How to Handle Cut Flowers

One of the joys of growing a flower garden is the luxury of being able to cut a bouquet to bring indoors. Many that you can grow easily are simply not available as cut flowers at the florist's shop. And what fun to choose flowers for the table to carry out a color scheme.

But there are tricks to all trades—including how to cut and keep fresh the flowers from your garden. Here are some tips regularly used by florists and experienced arrangers of homegrown blooms.

Like any art or craft, flower arranging requires good tools. But, in this case, the essentials are relatively few and inexpensive. All you really need, other than flowers, are three or four containers in basic shapes, needlepoint holders, a sharp scissors or knife, and the other simple items shown here.

Before going out into the garden to gather flowers, read these tips. They can make the difference between a professional, long-lasting bouquet and one that quickly wilts.

If you plan to cut only a few stems to bring right indoors, always carry them head-down. This keeps stems straight and prevents heavy flower heads from being snapped off.

It's important to get cut flowers into water as soon as possible after cutting. Cut stems at an angle and plunge into a pail of tepid water deep enough to come just short of flower heads. If putting several kinds into one pail, wrap each kind in sheets of newspaper first.

If you didn't carry a pail of water into the garden with you as you were cutting, re-snip each flower stem at an angle underwater before plunging into a pail of lukewarm water. Place the pail in a cool spot out of the sun, and let stand until the water cools to room temperature—for several hours or, preferably, overnight—before arranging the cut flowers. This step is called "conditioning."

If stems are thick or woody, use your sharp scissors or knife to make 1- or 2-inch slits from the bases upwards. This assures that they'll soak in enough water to keep blooms supplied with moisture. If you fail to do this, flowers and foliage will shortly go limp and probably will not revive.

Another important factor in the good looks and long life of your bouquet is your choice of flowers. Avoid buds so tight that they'll never open, as well as full blooms that will soon pass their prime.

The roses sketched below are good examples of a too-tight bud, a flower at the perfect stage for cutting, and a fully open flower that will soon wilt or shatter and spoil the appearance of your arrangement. Some flowers at this advanced stage may, however, be floated on water inside a rounded glass bowl and remain attractive for several days if you freshen water daily.

If you grow many roses, you will certainly want the pleasure of cutting some to bring indoors. But first, you must realize that the fate of future bloom depends on how you go about your cutting. Always leave at least two healthy five-leaflet leaves on the remaining stem to help the plant maintain vigor. If you cut very long stems, you probably will not have further bloom from them for the remainder of the rose season.

Another plant tempting to cut and bring indoors is the lily. Never cut a long stem, as the bulb needs the stem and foliage to form the strength to produce next year's bloom.

To assure the long life of your arrangement, be sure to place it where it is out of direct sunlight and protected from drafts—never in reach of air circulated by an air conditioner or a fan or the flower will dehydrate.

Flowers whose stems have been seared still need conditioning by being plunged into a pail of lukewarm water and left there for several hours or overnight.

To save pricked fingers when you're arranging roses, hold stems high and clip off thorns at the level you will touch in the process of arranging. For *all* cut flowers, clip off all foliage that would otherwise be below water level in the finished arrangement. Such leaves would quickly disintegrate, foul the water, and shorten the life of your arrangement. Always wash containers thoroughly after using them so they will be fresh and clean for the next arrangement.

Sometimes heavy-headed flowers such as large mums or dahlias bend over, nearly snapping off. You can perform surgery by taking a sturdy toothpick—the kind that's pointed at both ends—and, holding bent stem in an upright position, plunge the toothpick through the bloom center and down into the stem. Such blooms aren't long-lasting.

If you want to use garden lilies in a centerpiece for the dining table, it's good practice to snip off all pollen-bearing stamens of each bloom before you make the arrangement. Bits of stamen are apt to drop off and stain the flowers themselves, and—more important—the tablecloth below. These stains are persistent and hard to remove.

Many florists habitually cut off all such stamens on Easter lily plants before they are placed on sale. However, some lily-fanciers object to this practice on the grounds that it takes away from the natural beauty of the bloom.

Poppies, dahlias, and some other garden flowers with hollow stems or stems that exude a milky liquid on cutting need to be seared with a flame. The burner from your chafing pan or an old candle will do nicely. It's wise to take this step immediately after cutting. Carry the candle or other means of producing flame right into the garden with you and sear at once. If you cut stems shorter later, re-sear.

Roses and tulips open in a hurry once they're cut and brought indoors. To slow the opening, use florist's tape to gently hold the blooms shut until just before the arrangement is to be put on view. Also, slow the opening process by keeping the arrangement in a cool place until you're ready to display.

If you want to use some very wide-open chrysanthemums in a flower arrangement, use this tip to keep petals from dropping off in the handling process. Hold stems upside down and gently drip candle wax around the calyx—the outer circle of green that served to protect the flower when it was still in the bud stage. And a few drops of wax dripped into the bloom centers of flowers such as daylilies that tend to close early will help keep them open a bit longer.

Zones of Plant Hardiness

Throughout this book, we have referred to zone numbers that represent the northern limits of successful culture for certain plants.

Zone boundary lines are not absolute. You can expect temperatures to vary as much as 5° from those given on the opposite page. You must also consider localized conditions. Hills and valleys in certain areas do not always have the same high and low temperatures as those recorded at the official weather bureau stations.

Still other conditions to consider before selecting plants are rainfall, humidity, snow coverage, wind, and soil type. A specific perennial may survive in zone 3 in Maine, for example, but be completely unadapted to that same zone in North Dakota—simply because of differences in rainfall and humidity.

For assured success, start with local plant favorites. Your added care will help the natives prosper in domestic situations. And often they'll do better than plants brought in from distant places at surviving freakish weather, hail, flood, drought, or early and late frosts.

Be flexible. When certain plants prosper unexpectedly in your garden, consider adding more of them—perhaps in additional varieties or different colors. If others do poorly, don't hesitate to replace them with more hardy plants.

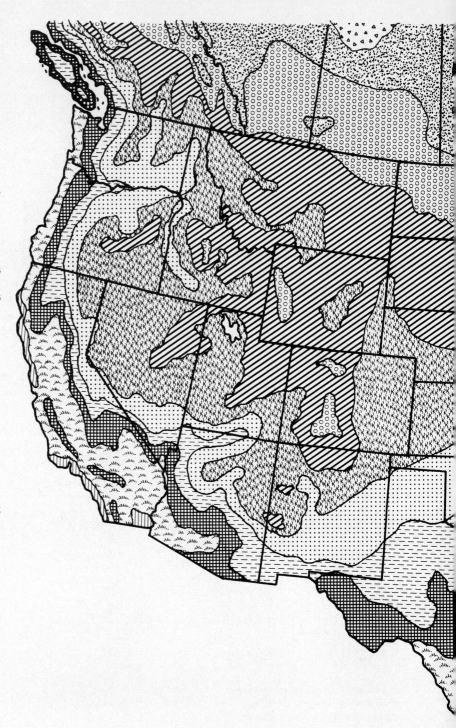

Source: United States Department of Agriculture

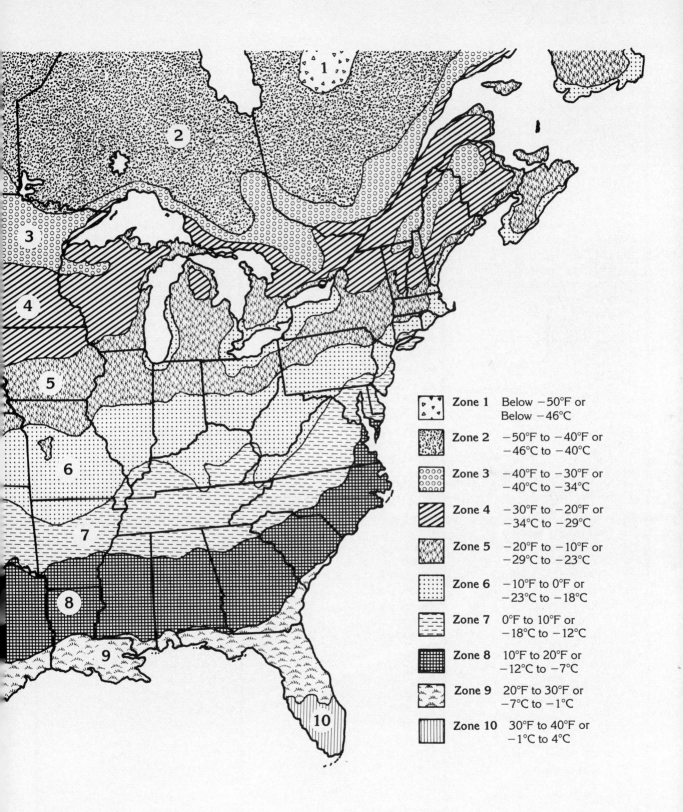

	Zone 1	Below −50°F or Below −46°C
	Zone 2	−50°F to −40°F or −46°C to −40°C
	Zone 3	−40°F to −30°F or −40°C to −34°C
	Zone 4	−30°F to −20°F or −34°C to −29°C
	Zone 5	−20°F to −10°F or −29°C to −23°C
	Zone 6	−10°F to 0°F or −23°C to −18°C
	Zone 7	0°F to 10°F or −18°C to −12°C
	Zone 8	10°F to 20°F or −12°C to −7°C
	Zone 9	20°F to 30°F or −7°C to −1°C
	Zone 10	30°F to 40°F or −1°C to 4°C

INDEX